PRAISE FOR *THE TV WRITER'S WORKBOOK*
by Ellen Sandler

"Ellen brings the same intelligence and humor to this book that she did to her *Everybody Loves Raymond* scripts, which made them so much fun to perform."
—Doris Roberts, Emmy Award–winning actress

"Ellen Sandler challenges you to develop your craft in order to exponentially grow your talent, then shows you how to do it and do it well. This book will make you a better, more confident writer. Plus, it's fun to read!"
—Pamela Jaye Smith, author of *Inner Drives: How to Write and Create Characters Using the Eight Classic Centers of Motivation*, www.mythworks.net

"What a fantastic book! It makes me wish I had become a TV writer—and has me believing I could actually do it. *The TV Writer's Workbook* is not only the most insightful and informative book available on writing for television; it's a funny, inspiring and wonderfully written guide that will take you—one step at a time—all the way to a terrific script and a successful television career."
—Michael Hauge, author of *Writing Screenplays That Sell*

"Ellen Sandler is a TV writer's best friend. It's like having a story editor on your shoulder, whispering you through your script and mentoring your entire career."
—Signe Olynyk, President/CEO of the Great American PitchFest

"Ellen Sandler is funny! This book is fun, and it's chock-full of specifics about the industry and writing. Anyone who wants to write absolutely needs this book!"
—Dr. Linda Seger, author of *Making a Good Script Great*

"Veteran showrunner Ellen Sandler has created an ingenious method to teach aspiring scribes how to navigate the madness that keeps the television machine running. An important and entertaining primer on how to construct your first episodic script, Ms. Sandler's book is a rich resource filled with comic wit and refreshing candor—exactly what you'd expect from the co-executive producer of the Emmy Award–winning classic, *Everybody Loves Raymond.*"
—Georgia Jeffries, associate professor, Writing Division, USC School of Cinematic Arts

"A complete, concise, comprehensive guide to writing for television . . . warm, heartfelt, honest, and a joy to read. There is no better way for an aspiring writer to learn to write for television than from someone who has actually done it."
—Sheldon Bull, author of *Elephant Bucks: An Insider's Guide to Writing for TV Sitcoms;* writer, director, and producer of *Coach, Newhart,* and *Sabrina the Teenage Witch*

"If writing for television is your passion and you aren't sure what to do, buy Ellen Sandler's *The TV Writer's Workbook.* Ellen provides you with an honest, 'in-the-trenches' look at what it takes to make it as a writer in the highly competitive world of TV. This book is a guaranteed investment in your writing career."
—Kathie Fong Yoneda, author of *The Script-Selling Game: A Hollywood Insider's Look at Getting Your Script Sold and Produced*

"Why did it take Ellen Sandler so long to write this fantastic book? Maybe if this book had been around when I was starting out I'd have a much bigger house with a much better view."
—Rob Lotterstein, creator/executive producer of Fox's *The War at Home*

THE TV WRITER'S WORKBOOK

A Creative Approach
to Television Scripts

ELLEN SANDLER

DELTA TRADE PAPERBACKS

THE TV WRITER'S WORKBOOK
A Delta Trade Paperback / April 2007

Published by
Bantam Dell
A Division of Random House, Inc.
New York, New York

Author photo by Christiane Covington, www.covingtonphotography.com

Book design by Sabrina Bowers

Delta is a registered trademark of Random House, Inc., and the colophon
is a trademark of Random House, Inc.

Library of Congress Cataloging-in-Publication Data

Sandler, Ellen.
The TV writer's workbook : a creative approach to television scripts /
Ellen Sandler.
p. cm.
"A Delta trade paperback."
Includes index.
ISBN: 978-0-385-34050-2 (trade pbk.)
1. Television authorship. I. Title. II. Title: Television writer's workbook.
PM1992.7 .S35 2007
808/2′25—dc22
2006039762

Printed in the United States of America
Published simultaneously in Canada

www.bantamdell.com

BVG 10 9 8 7

"All journeys have secret destinations of which the traveler is unaware."
— MARTIN BUBER,
1878–1965, PHILOSOPHER

Contents

Acknowledgments

In Chapter 20 of this book I say that in this business nobody does it alone. I not only say it, I show it written in stone. It has been true of my whole career and it is certainly true of this book. Though my name is on the cover, it took the contributions of many people to bring this book into existence. I am not a good enough writer to sufficiently thank them in mere words, but I hope seeing their name in print will be a small indication of how grateful I am for their contributions and support.

Thank you to the showrunners I have worked for (including the ones who fired me), my writing partners (including the ones who left me), and my colleagues on staff (especially the ones who made me laugh), from whom I have learned whatever I know about discipline, determination, and how to tell a good story.

Thanks to Bruce Brown at Innovative Artists, my agent of many years, who guided my career and made the deals that gave me the opportunity to write for TV. He also made sure I told the truth in the agents chapter. He is an excellent human being and friend, qualities thought to be nonexistent in a Hollywood agent.

I promised him I would never reveal this, but I'm told no one reads the aknowledgments, so I assume his secret is still safe.

Thanks to Jessica Weiner, who first said write a book and somehow made me think I actually could. To Mary Lengle, who put me on track. To Kathie Fong Yoneda for reading my proposal and confirming that I had something to say. To Erin Clermont for getting me through the first draft when I thought I would drown.

Thanks to Dan and Michele for the lovely solitude in the room overlooking the Hudson where I finished this book. To my therapist(s) past and present—no names; they don't like to take credit. (That's part of the therapy, taking responsibility for one's own actions.)

Thanks to Adam Peck of Synchronicity Management and Jen Good, Senior Agent at Metropolitan Agency, for their invaluable additions to the chapter on agents and managers.

Thanks to HBO for permission to reprint the "No Fat" episode of *Everybody Loves Raymond* and to Michael Wright and his helpful staff there for making it happen. To *Written By* and Marsha Scarborough for permission to reprint her excellent article about the making of "No Fat." To Patricia Nelson at Fish & Richardson for copyright information.

Thanks to Judy Carter, who made me a teacher when she asked me to create a pitching workshop for her Comedy Conference. And to Larry Kohn for turning me into a coach.

Thanks to Linda Venis at The Writers' Program of UCLA Extension, who gave me the opportunity to teach and learn so much of what is in this book. To Susan Golant, who taught the UCLA Extension class on How to Write a Book Proposal, where I learned what I needed to know to get this project started.

Thanks to Shannon Jamieson Vazquez, who, when she saw that book proposal, believed there was a book here.

Thanks to my editor at Bantam, Philip Rappaport, who patiently walked me through the whole process and who impatiently insisted I meet my deadlines (almost).

Thanks to Speed Weed for introducing me to his sister, Elisabeth Weed, my wonderful book agent, who proves that someone who is beautiful with long legs and naturally blond hair can also be one hell of a negotiator. Her enthusiasm and encouragement for this book have been unending.

Thanks to Ealeana Ostrem, my assistant, who has, when necessary, even been willing to neglect her dog for my benefit. If it's true that God is in the details, she must be divine, because she picks up every one. Without her, very little would ever actually happen and this book would be at least a hundred pages longer and much more confusing.

Thanks to my students and clients who provided many of the examples I use in this book. Their courage and passion to write constantly inspire and teach me far more than I ever teach them.

Most of all, thanks to my family:

My daughter, Molly Danziger, for suggesting I come to Tacoma, Washington, where she goes to college, to write this book. She was so right. I would never have found the time or concentration needed to write this book at home in Los Angeles. Plus, looking forward to dinner with her every night made my twelve-hour workdays a lot easier.

My son, Max Danziger, who, thirteen years ago when he was only eight, said to me, "If you try to be perfect, you'll wind up being less than good," which has turned out to be the very best advice on writing (and everything else, for that matter) that anyone has ever given me. He also told me I had to finish the book because at least twenty of his friends want to buy it.

My husband, Peter Basch, who is always there to catch me

ACKNOWLEDGMENTS

when I falter—okay, not always, but more than I ever expected anyone would be. He supports me in everything I do, all day, every day, be it tech or emotional, and hardly ever complains.

Thank you, all. Thank you, thank you, thank you.

Introduction

My goal for this book is to tell you the truth about writing for television.

Here's the first truth: There is only one way to get a job writing television—no, it's not by getting the right agent. The way to get work is by having written something fresh and wonderful that people get excited about.

It is just that simple.

Simple, but not easy.

No one can teach you how to write, but you can learn it—by writing. That's why I call this book a workbook. You must actually do the work.

You watch TV, you know *what* a good show is, but if you are reading this book, I assume you would also like to know *how* to write a good show. This book focuses on the process. It provides you with a procedure to follow, guidelines for television form, and techniques to avoid stumbling blocks. These tools will get you to the page not only with greater frequency but with more focus and control, i.e., craft.

For the past twenty years I have been involved in the writing, reading, evaluating, and rewriting of television scripts, my own and those of many other writers. What I've discovered is that everyone has talent, but that talent is pretty useless without craft. However, craft is learnable. You can practice craft, and you can get better at it. Then, magically, as your craft improves, your talent grows exponentially.

No one, including you, knows how much talent you have until you develop the techniques that give your talent a way to flow. Craft gives you control, and gaining control of your talent will give you the courage to trust your instincts. Every time you do an exercise—without judgment and for its own sake—you will be developing instincts and confidence. You will be *en*couraged. And courage is what you need to pursue writing.

The principles and exercises in this book are not meant to be the only way, but rather *one* way. You can do them on any level. Use them, adapt them, change them, but just plain do the work, and you will discover your own process. You will *learn* to write a television script. If I did it, you can too. I am not a genius. I am not even a great writer. What I am is a person who got a lot of help from a lot of people, learned the form, and did the work. I became a pretty good writer and I got paid to do it. So can you.

With a couple of friends in both low and high places, the courage to grab opportunities, and the humility to be grateful for what comes your way, you can find both money and personal satisfaction in the work of writing for television.

In this book I want to give you the encouragement and hope I know you will need. I also want to give you respect for what it takes to make a career in an exciting, high-paying, but tremendously competitive and elusive field—in other words, the truth about writing for television, or at least the truth as I see it. If that sounds like what you want to know, then I think we're good to go.

"HOW I GOT INTO TV"

FADE IN:

INT. PALATIAL HOLLYWOOD HOME — DAY

Pretentiously decorated, obviously a set. No
one actually lives here.

Framed EMMY NOMINATION CERTIFICATE too prominently displayed. Russian wolfhound lounges
nearby, indicating "important authoress."

Television writer/producer ELLEN SANDLER, wearing a gray Armani suit, sits in a large throne-
like chair in front of huge Masterpiece Theatre
fireplace and reads a script. Fake fire blazes,
despite the fact that it's . . .

EXT. LOS ANGELES — DAY — AERIAL SHOT OF THE CITY

Tops of buildings obscured and the Hollywood
sign barely visible through dense, dirty smog.

OUTDOOR THERMOMETER

It reads eighty-seven degrees and climbing.

That's right, hot and smoggy.

                              BACK TO:
PALATIAL HOLLYWOOD HOME

ELLEN looks up from the script.

                ELLEN
        I've been writing for television
        since "Taxi" was on the air. In
        fact, writing for "Taxi" was my
        first TV job.

THEME from "Taxi" plays.

FLASHBACK — NEW YORK CITY (early '80s)

                ELLEN (V.O.)
        I was working off-off Broadway.

EXT. HORRIBLE STOREFRONT THEATER — DAY

A narrow building, sandwiched between a bagel
shop and a discount wig store. Posters tacked
up on the windows advertise "New Works by New
Playwrights." 25 YEARS YOUNGER ELLEN — long
hair, jeans — struggles to balance a pile of
scripts under one arm while she opens the three
padlocks on the steel door.

                ELLEN (V.O.)
        Way off-off Broadway. You can't
        see or hear it from here, but,

> believe me, the toilet in that
> place hasn't worked properly in
> twenty years. I didn't care be-
> cause that's where I was writing
> and directing plays.

FEMALE HAND OPENS PLAY SCRIPT.

Distinct stage play formatting — lots of dialogue, single spaced, narrow margins, no slug
lines or descriptions.

> ELLEN (V.O.)
> In other words, for love.

FEMALE HANDS OPEN A WALLET.

No bills. Couple of pennies and a nickel.

Small piece of lint.

> ELLEN (V.O.)
> And then a one act play I'd been
> working on got produced . . . in
> Los Angeles.

EXT. BLUE SKY — DAY

A paper airplane flies through the air, sailing
past fluffy white clouds . . .

INT. INSTITUTIONAL HALLWAY

. . . and floats down to land on a grubby beige
linoleum floor. The same female hands pick up
the paper airplane and unfold it, revealing a
theater program. It reads:

A ONE ACT PLAY FESTIVAL

                    ELLEN (V.O.)
          It was performed at the geograph-
          ically undesirable location of
          Vermont and Melrose avenues.

EXT. L.A. CITY COLLEGE — DAY

Single-story institutional square building,
huge Seal of the City of Los Angeles on the
side, only steps away from the constant
whizzing traffic of low-rent Vermont Avenue.

                    ELLEN (V.O.)
          Couldn't have been more small-
          time. But, after two dozen
          rewrites, the script really
          worked . . .

INT. BLACK BOX THEATER — NIGHT

The set on stage consists of a blue backdrop
that reads "YANKEE STADI-" and a polished
chrome turnstile representing an entrance to
the stadium.

                    ELLEN (V.O.)
          The actors were terrific . . .

Rhea Perlman sits on a blanket spread out on
the stage floor. She wears jeans, a Yankee baseball shirt and cap, and eats a handful of Cap'n
Crunch cereal directly from the box.

The play referred to above was *Pennant Fever* and it was the result of a col-
laboration between Ellen Sandler and Dennis Danziger. Ms. Sandler was
credited as the director, Mr. Danziger as the writer.

It's twenty-five years ago, "Cheers" does not exist yet, she's hardly a household name at this time.

She's playing ANGELA, a girl who loves baseball and is scared of nothing.

Lee Wilkof ENTERS stage left.

Lee is short and, though only twenty-six at the time, balding. He will one day be nominated for a Tony for his work in the Broadway revival of "Guys and Dolls." But right now, he is unknown and playing JOEL, an intellectual grad student who's afraid of everything, especially baseball and girls.

> RHEA AS ANGELA
> Not another step!

> LEE AS JOEL
> (terrified)
> Yeeks, sorry to frighten you.

Audience laughter, distinctly live and un-canned.

> ELLEN (V.O.)
> The show started with a big laugh
> and ran . . .
> > DISSOLVE TO:

LATER

LAUGHTER and loud APPLAUSE as the actors bow.

> ELLEN (V.O.)
> . . . for 39 fast and funny min-utes. The audience loved it.

INT. LOBBY — CONTINUOUS

Actually not a lobby at all: a hallway with
gray cinder-block walls, and that grubby beige
linoleum floor.

> ELLEN (V.O.)
> Conventional wisdom was that im-
> portant showbiz types would not
> go east of La Cienega but Jim
> Brooks, creator of "The Mary
> Tyler Moore Show," now the
> Executive Producer of "Taxi" and
> soon to be writer/producer/direc-
> tor of "Broadcast News," "Terms
> of Endearment," "Jerry Maguire,"
> and "The Simpsons" — in other
> words, a Comedy God — is here.

JIM BROOKS ENTERS the lobby, laughing and talking with a YOUNGER DANNY DEVITO.

> ELLEN (V.O.)
> DeVito was Rhea's boyfriend and,
> as I'm sure you remember, was
> then playing Louie on "Taxi." He
> brought Brooks to see Rhea in the
> play.

JIM BROOKS rushes over to 25 YEARS YOUNGER
ELLEN, who is surrounded by supportive friends
and admiring strangers.

> JIM BROOKS
> (wildly enthusiastic)
> You're terrific! I want you to
> write for "Taxi."

JIM BROOKS hands 25 YEARS YOUNGER ELLEN his card.

>   JIM BROOKS
>   Call me Monday.

And he's gone.

>   ELLEN (V.O.)
>   Just like in the movies, huh?

25 YEARS YOUNGER ELLEN, dazed, looks at the
card . . .

BACK TO: PALATIAL HOLLYWOOD HOME

ELLEN leans in to the camera with a big grin.

>   ELLEN
>   And that's when I started writing
>   for money.

The phony living room set crumbles behind
ELLEN, and when the dust settles she is
in . . .

INT. ELLEN'S HOME OFFICE — DAY

A sunny room. Utilitarian and simple. Office
Depot was the decorator. White Formica desk,
open laptop computer, lots of books, piles of
scripts.

Cardboard file boxes stacked on the red Mexican
tile floor.

A scruffy brown mutt sleeps on the worn sofa.

ELLEN, in gray sweats, swivels in her desk
chair to face the camera.

                    ELLEN
          The point is that I had no idea
          how to get into TV, I just wrote
          stuff and got it done. Somewhere.
          Anywhere. Nowhere big. Just done.
          And I didn't know anybody impor-
          tant, at least I didn't think I
          did — Rhea Perlman was an actress
          I knew from my days working in
          those off-off Broadway theaters
          with the bad toilets. Who knew
          she knew somebody who knew some-
          body?

ELLEN picks up a script from her desk and leafs
through it.

                    ELLEN (CONT'D)
          I learned to write by doing it
          and eventually my writing got
          good, and I got lucky. Somebody
          noticed.

ELLEN looks directly to the camera.

                    ELLEN (CONT'D)
          But then I really had to learn
          what I was doing to stay in the
          game. That's what's in this book.
          Things like how to meet people
          when you're shy, or how to write
          a cover letter to someone you
          want to impress. I'll tell you
          the tricks I use to beat my inner
          procrastinator — yes, I have one,
          and I bet mine's bigger than
          yours. I've also found creative
          ways to make a story both per-
          sonal and professional, and I'll

tell you how to recognize the red
flags that mean you've gotta do
better. In other words, I'll tell
you what I've learned and my hope
is that some of it will work for
you too.

                    FADE OUT.

But not . . .

            THE END

PART I

What You Need to Know

1. THE SPEC SCRIPT

No one (I hope) watches television all the time, but everyone watches it sometimes. Television is pervasive and common, in the sense of communal, familiar, and available to all. Television establishes our ethical, moral, social, and, God knows, material boundaries more than any other factor in modern life. More than the movies, more than politics—no wonder you want to write for it. It's powerful!

Because it is common, television is often dismissed as insignificant, unworthy of respect or care. Because it is pervasive it is voracious—television needs material, and it reproduces like an amoeba, constantly dividing and replicating itself to fill the continuing void.

Television needs more, and it needs it now. That's where you come in. Your job as a writer is to supply it with content. This leads to fast, which leads to sloppy, which leads to formulaic, writing.

"It's not brain surgery," you'll often hear people in the industry say about working in TV. As a way to deflate self-importance, it's a perfectly good sentiment, but resist the impulse to use it as an excuse to lower standards; because in a way, when you create for TV you *are* doing a kind of brain surgery. You are shaping people's perceptions, and affecting their reality.

A career as a writer in Hollywood begins with excellent writing (excellent by commercial standards—we'll get into that in a minute). After that it's about persistence, tenacity, and some luck, though less than you might think. These are not secrets. Everybody knows the rules. The secret is committing to them. That's what makes a career happen.

In order to write for TV, you must get a job. In order to get a job, you must have material to show that you can write. Usually that will be a spec script.

What Is a Spec Script?

A television spec script is an unsolicited, original episode written for an established TV show. No money, no contract, no guarantees. In all likelihood, a spec script will never be sold or produced. What it will be is READ. That's what you write it for: to be read by as many people connected to show business as you can get it to. Everyone counts. You never know who knows someone who knows someone.

There are two different kinds of spec scripts, one for TV and one for film. You write a spec screenplay when you are not established enough to get a deal to write a screenplay based on a pitch. You write a spec screenplay and hold on to the dream that a studio will pay you for the rights to make it into a movie. Or, more likely, pay you for the rights to change it completely and never make it into a movie, but at least you get a check. You can sell a spec screenplay.

A television spec script is different. You don't write a TV spec with the expectation of selling it to the show. It could happen, it has happened—it's Hollywood, everything happens once or twice—and if it happens to you, great! Call your lawyer and make sure you're protected on the back end. (Not as sexy as it sounds, but even more exciting; see Showbiz Meanings for Regular Words: A Selective Glossary.) But what's much more likely, and therefore what we'll be talking about in this book, is that you'll write a spec TV episode to prove that you can do the work. It's a writing sample, a portfolio piece. In film, people are looking for a script, but in TV they are looking for a *writer.*

Why Write for TV?

I teach scriptwriting classes and when I ask students why they want to write a spec script, I usually get an answer like, "It's fun." Well, that's great, but that won't get you to the end of your script because a lot about writing isn't so much fun. A lot of it is frustrating, confusing, and downright hard.

So they think about it and I hear, "To tell a story" or "To make people laugh." I've even heard, "Because I really, really, really want to." All of those are good reasons to write something, but not necessarily a TV spec script.

The only reason to write a television episodic spec script is: money. When I teach, I usually draw a big **$** on the whiteboard and everybody laughs. I suppose because that's what they were really thinking but were afraid to say. Or maybe they were even afraid to think it. Maybe they feel it's not a worthy reason to write. But the truth is that television is a commercial medium and you write it for money.

There's a story about George Bernard Shaw, who in the '30s came to Hollywood for a meeting with Samuel Goldwyn, the head of MGM. Goldwyn wanted the rights to Shaw's plays, but, naturally, wanted to pay as little as possible for them. Goldwyn went on and on about what a genius Shaw was, how much he admired his plays, what a great artist he was, and how he, Goldwyn, was also a great artist and that he, in fact, would rather make a great artistic picture than eat a good meal. Shaw finally got up, thanked Goldwyn for the meeting, but respectfully declined to sell him the rights. Goldwyn was stunned: "Why not?" Shaw replied, "The trouble, sir, is that you are interested only in art, while I am interested only in money."

Form Versus Formula

What writing for money means is that when you sit down to write you have to follow the rules. By rules, I don't mean formula—*formula* is what makes a writer a hack, and leads to predictable, dull scripts that nobody wants to read past page 8. However, there is *form*—quite a different thing. Television scripts have a specific form, and you must follow it.

It doesn't matter if you think you know how to do it better or funnier than what's on the air. That's not your job when you're writing a spec script. Your job is to do it exactly the way it's done and *still* be original. If you follow the rules without originality, your work will be okay but it will not distinguish itself as special.

Yes, you're writing for money, but you are not writing *only* for money. You must also put some art into your commercial product. It's very unlikely that you'll ever get to write for money if you don't put something of yourself into your script. The richest, most successful television writers I know have all written commercially savvy products from a personal point of view. Creative with the form? No. Creative with the content? Yes.

On any given day on any given reader's desk (or more likely, on the floor) there are going to be three piles of scripts. The piles will look like this:

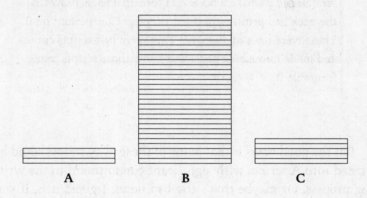

Pile A, the smallest one, will be, as you probably guessed, the good scripts. The ones with a story we care about, dialogue that jumps up off the page, something very special that's worth noting. These are the scripts that will get passed along with "Recommend" written on the coverage form.

Pile C will be the hopelessly bad scripts—handwritten, incorrectly formatted, offensive, plagiarized, and so forth.

And Pile B, the one that rises endlessly to the ceiling? That is what I call the Big Pile of Okay. Scripts that look like scripts, read like scripts, and might even have some pretty good laughs. There's nothing really wrong with them, but there's nothing really right with them either. This, in my experience of reading scripts (I've read thousands, honestly), and in the experience of everyone else I know who reads scripts for a living, is the category that the vast majority of scripts fall into. I don't think I need to tell you where these scripts are going; suffice to say they are not going on to anyone else's desk.

> **Once, in an agent's waiting room,** I picked up a scratch pad to make a note. As I tore off a page, I saw that the back had printing in the distinctive Courier font on it. These were lines of dialogue! This agent had scripts cut up and made into memo pads! You know those scripts came from Pile B.

But the good news is that many of these okay scripts could be turned into A scripts with significant commitment to the writing process. Or maybe that's the bad news; I guess it is, if you thought writing for TV was going to be easy.

The exercises in this book are tools to guide you in following the form and infusing it with your own original creative force. That will get you from the Big Pile of Okay to Recommend.

And if you can do that, you can probably get paid to write TV.

What Show Should You Spec?

Write a show you love to watch. That, in my opinion, is the single most important factor in choosing a show to write. Don't write a spec of a show you don't like, even if someone in the industry has told you it's the hot show to write.* When you get to pick, and your spec may be the only time you have that opportunity, by all means be picky. Only write a show that you relate to, a show you like to watch, with characters you care about. That is first and foremost—but it's not the only criterion.

Here are three other factors to keep in mind when choosing a show to write for.

1. The show must be on the air now

This is a rule. Don't write a *Friends* spec, even if you saw every episode and you have the greatest idea for a Rachel story ever. Anything that is off the air is an old show, even if it went off yesterday and the reruns are playing every day.

There's a story that's been circulating around Hollywood for years—you may have heard it—about somebody who wrote a great episode of the old *Dick Van Dyke Show* and people thought it was so gutsy and original that the writer got a lot of interest.

First of all, I don't believe that really happened—I believe someone did it, I just don't believe it got them work—and secondly, if it is true, then it's been done and no longer has any value as a gutsy original move.

So please, write only a show that's on the air.

---

*The "liking factor" does not apply when you are offered a job or a chance to pitch. If someone wants to pay you to write a show, or even wants to think about paying you but you don't like the show, you *find* something to like about it, and you *write* it, especially when you're at an early stage in your career. Later, when you have more than one offer, you can hold out for a show you actually do like.

In fact, any show that's been on the air more than five years is probably too old to write a spec for, even if it's not going off the air for a couple more seasons. If you're sending out an episode of an old show, the feeling is that you're not fresh, not current, not keeping up with the trends, and in TV, that is death.

2. It should be a hit show
Here's why:

- A hit show is not likely to be canceled the day before you finish your spec script.

- People who will be reading your spec will be familiar with the show and the characters.

- A hit is a hit because it works. A show that works will be easier to write and will make a much better sample. One of the reasons you write a spec is to benefit and learn from a more experienced writer who created a successful show.

- Hits are copied. There will be new shows like it on the air, and those are shows that will be looking for staff. If you've written a spec of the show they've cloned, it will be an excellent sample to demonstrate how appropriate you would be for their show.

What defines a hit? It used to be that only shows in the top 10 were hits, but that's changed. In these days of more viewer choices and lower network ratings, it isn't always obvious what constitutes a hit, but numbers are still the first guide. Check the weekly rankings.* To be considered a hit, a commercial network show should be in the top 25 to 30 on the list.

---

*The weekly Nielsen rankings are published on Wednesdays in the Calendar section of the *Los Angeles Times,* also in *Daily Variety* and *The Hollywood Reporter.* Oddly, the whole list is not shown online at the Nielsen website; they show only the top 10. (www.nielsenmedia.com)

You aren't limited to prime-time network programming to find on-air hit shows to write. Another reliable gauge for spec script status is awards. If a show has been nominated for Emmys, Golden Globes, or any of the various Guild* awards, it's a mark that the industry is aware of the show and respects it.

Shows like *Monk* (USA Network), *Veronica Mars* (CW), *Weeds* (Showtime), *The Shield* (fX), *The Closer* (TNT), and *The Office* (NBC) may not pull big ratings, but they have won multiple nominations for their stars and writers, which raises their profile and makes them viable choices for your spec.

3. You have a connection

You went to acting school with someone in the cast, your roommate's buddy is an assistant editor on the show, or your cousin knows a production assistant's life partner. If you have a genuine connection, no matter how minor, it could be a big help. For one thing, it will be easier to get scripts of the show to study, and you'll find out why that's crucial in the next chapter. If it's a multi-camera show, they shoot in front of a live audience, and your connection can get you seats for a taping and maybe even an introduction after the shoot. If it's a single-camera show, you may be able to get an invite to the set to observe.

The most important advantage is the possibility of getting your spec read by a writer on the show and a chance for some professional feedback—and, who knows, maybe even a recommendation to that writer's agent or the showrunner. But don't expect that; just ask for feedback.

---

*The Screen Actors Guild (www.sagawards.com), Writers Guild (www.wga.org), and Directors Guild (www.dga.org) all give coveted television awards—you can go to the websites to check nominees and winners both current and from the past few seasons.

Many people will advise you not to write a spec of a show you want to write for, because you won't write it as well as the writers do and they'll pick it apart. There's some truth to this; however, I think that if you know someone in any capacity at a show, the chance to get expert feedback is too good an opportunity to pass up. You might not get hired there, but you're likely to have a much-improved spec script to show to everybody else.

4. Again, write a show you like

This is so important it bears repeating. Even if a show meets all of the above criteria perfectly, if you don't like the show and you don't enjoy watching it, you won't write a great spec script. So find a show you like and that also meets most, if not all, of the above guidelines, and that's the show you should spec.

What if the show you love doesn't fit any of the other requirements? My grandma always told me, "It's just as easy to fall in love with a rich man as a poor one." It applies here. Wouldn't it be just as easy to love a show that meets the other requirements too? Or maybe not. My best friend fell in love with a guy who had no money when she married him and now he's a multimillionaire, they have three houses, and she's got pearls the size of golf balls. So sometimes if you ignore the good advice and just follow your heart, it works out okay. But then, that's real life—which is a lot less predictable than television.

Once you've chosen a show, you've started the engine, but where are you going? What's your next step?

2. READ TO WRITE

You've picked a show you love, so of course you've watched it. You may have watched every episode, you may have even TiVo'd them and watched them several times. That's great, that will help, but you are still not familiar with your show from a writer's perspective. And you need to be, because you are not writing a *show*, you are writing a *script*. There's a difference.

Think of a show as a finished house where people slam doors (if it's a family drama), run up the stairs (a police procedural), or flush the toilets (comedy). Then think of the script as the architect's blueprint that lets you build that house and feel confident it will withstand all those activities. If you build that house without a blueprint—say, from a picture in *Architectural Digest*—how sturdy is it going to be? That's what you're doing if you construct a television spec script of a show just from watching it on the air.

You need to *read* scripts. You need to see how your show lays out on the page. If you write a show based only on how it looks on TV, you'll get some of the style and probably even the voices of the characters, but you will miss finding the substance of the show. You will not have an instinctive understanding of how that show tells stories. Your script will read like an imitation of that show and it will feel hollow.

How I Learned to Read

Back in the '70s, when I was working in ill-equipped, off-off-Broadway theaters for love, I got a job working as a reader for the legendary Joseph Papp,* the founder of the renowned Public Theatre. Joe, as he was known to absolutely everyone, was, at that time, the bright light of the American theater. Every new play written in English passed through his office.

Joe had great reverence for writers. He knew they were the lifeblood of the theater and he wanted every submission read, synopsized, and evaluated. I got $10 a script, so you can imagine how many plays I had to read in order to pay rent and buy bagels.

I didn't make a lot of money, but I got something of lifelong value. I learned the value of reading with purpose. I learned to read for story and character, to synopsize theme and plot, and to see potential in the midst of confusion. I couldn't get away with a bland "I like it" or even a vigorous "I hate it" in my evaluations. I had to think and analyze and then put into words what I thought, and it had to be short so Joe could get it quickly. I learned to write clearly and to the point. As an added benefit, I learned to write fast. (Being paid by the piece will do that for you.)

---

*Joe Papp gave Meryl Streep, Raul Julia, Mandy Patinkin, Dianne Weist, and many others their first notable roles. He produced the most significant plays and influential productions in the American theater of the '60s and '70s, among them *Hair* and *A Chorus Line* (Pulitzer Prize), and he provided a home to many emerging writers, including Sam Shepard, David Rabe, and David Mamet.

Reading with Purpose

Reading scripts is essential for commercial television writing, because you must present your work in a style and form that is recognizable to the industry. The possibility of getting hired to write for television is directly related to your ability to produce original ideas in a familiar form.

The way to get to know the form is to read scripts. Not just once, but many times, and with purpose. You need to analyze them and get inside the structure. You will find suggestions on where to get these scripts in Appendix III: Sources.

When I went to work on the series *Coach,* the first day of the new season, Alan Kirshenbaum, the showrunner, gathered all the writers in his office and laid out what was expected of us. We were to pitch story ideas, read and make notes on every script in production, go to all run-throughs, be at the table for every rewrite session, and show up on the floor for shoot night. But most of all, our job was—and he actually yelled this at us—"TO WRITE DRAFTS!!"

What every showrunner wants from you is a good first draft, and that means a good story. The writing staff will sharpen the dialogue, punch up the jokes, and trim the fat at the rewrite table, but no amount of punch-up can fix a story that isn't working. You learn to tell stories that work by getting inside the structure of the scripts.

How do you do that? Well, here's how I do it: I make a chart and I count everything I can think of to count. There are examples of the kind of things I put on my chart on the following pages. The items on my sample chart are by no means definitive, because there *is* no definitive list. These are some basics to get you started. Adapt the chart to suit your show by adding appropriate categories and skipping those that don't apply to your show.

For instance, my sample chart shows a page count by acts and by scenes using the letter designations common to sitcom format. But a single-camera drama will have four, five, or even six acts rather than two and there will be many scenes of variable lengths. In film format you count scene length in increments of $1/8$ of a page.* So, let's use an example of a *Grey's Anatomy* script in which Act I runs $14^5/8$ pages and has 16 scenes. When I break those scenes down I find that four scenes run $1/4$ of a page, three scenes run $1/2$ of a page, one scene runs $3/4$ of a page, two run 1 page, one runs $1^1/4$ pages, two run $1^1/2$ pages, two run $1^5/8$ pages, and one runs $1^7/8$ pages. I would enter these numbers into my chart and after I had done three scripts like this I would have a good idea of how my own Act I should break down. If I then discover that my Act I has only 10 scenes and many of them run over 2 pages, I'm not telling my story in the show's rhythm and it won't feel like a *Grey's Anatomy* script. I've included a partial single-camera chart that suggests how to configure single-camera scene counting.†

---

*An increment of $1/8$ of a page is the standard count used by production managers to calculate time allotments for production shooting schedules. For your breakdown purposes you could choose to simplify and just use $1/4$, $1/2$, and $3/4$ pages as your standard. For you, the writer, it's not about the math as much as it is about the basic patterns that the script falls into.
†If you come up with another way, please go to my website (www .SandlerInk.com), where you can email me your suggestion.

EPISODIC TELEVISION SCRIPT BREAKDOWN CHART

Multi-Camera Half Hour Comedy Format

	Script 1	Script 2	Script 3
# of Acts			
# of pages per script			
# of pages Act I			
# of pages Act II			
# of scenes in episode			
# of scenes Act I			
# of scenes Act II			
# of pages in Teaser			
# of pages in Scene A			
# of pages in Scene B			
# of pages in Scene C			
# of pages in Scene D			
# of pages in Scene E			
# of pages in Scene H*			
# of pages in Scene J			
# of pages in Tag			
# of scenes Character A is in			
# of scenes Character B is in			
# of scenes Character C is in			
# of scenes Character D is in			

*See Scene Numbering Sitcom Style in Chapter 12: The Outline for an explanation of skipped letters.

	Script 1	Script 2	Script 3
# of scenes Character E is in			
# of Guest Characters			
# of scenes Guest Character is in			
# of lines Guest Character has			
# of sets used			
# of times regular set A used			
# of times regular set B used			
# of times regular set C used			
Where is the opening scene set			
Who is in the opening scene			
# of swing sets*			
# of times swing set is used			
# of jokes on a page			
# of scenes the Lead has the last line			
# of scenes Character B has last line			
# of scenes another character has last line			
If a character has a trademark line, # of times he or she says it			
# of scenes with Lead and one other character			
# of scenes with all the regular characters together			
# of days in the episode			

*See Showbiz Meanings for Regular Words: A Selective Glossary.

	Script 1	Script 2	Script 3
Scene that introduces the problem of the story			
# of scenes that Lead enters after the scene starts			
# of times Lead insults or argues with another character			

EPISODIC TELEVISION SCRIPT BREAKDOWN CHART

Single-Camera Film Format

	Script 1	Script 2	Script 3
# of Acts			
# of pages per script			
# of pages Act I			
# of pages Act II			
# pages Act III			
# pages Act IV			
# scenes in episode			
# scenes Act I			
#$1/_8$ page scenes			
#$1/_4$ page scenes			
#$1/_2$ page scenes			
#$3/_4$ page scenes			
#1 page scenes			
#$1 1/_8$ page scenes			
#$1 1/_4$ page scenes			

	Script 1	Script 2	Script 3
#1$^{1}/_{2}$ page scenes			
#1$^{3}/_{4}$ page scenes			
#2+ page scenes			
# scenes Act II			
#$^{1}/_{8}$ page scenes			
#$^{1}/_{4}$ page scenes			
#$^{1}/_{2}$ page scenes			
#$^{3}/_{4}$ page scenes			
#1 page scenes			
#1$^{1}/_{8}$ page scenes			
#1$^{1}/_{4}$ page scenes			
#1$^{1}/_{2}$ page scenes			
#1$^{3}/_{4}$ page scenes			
#2+ page scenes			
# scenes Act III			
#$^{1}/_{8}$ page scenes			
#$^{1}/_{4}$ page scenes			
#$^{1}/_{2}$ page scenes			
#$^{3}/_{4}$ page scenes			
#1 page scenes			
#1$^{1}/_{8}$ page scenes			
#1$^{1}/_{4}$ page scenes			
#1$^{1}/_{2}$ page scenes			
#1$^{3}/_{4}$ page scenes			
#2+ page scenes			

	Script 1	Script 2	Script 3
# scenes Act IV			
#$1/_8$ page scenes			
#$1/_4$ page scenes			
#$1/_2$ page scenes			
#$3/_4$ page scenes			
#1 page scenes			
#$1^1/_8$ page scenes			
#$1^1/_4$ page scenes			
#$1^1/_2$ page scenes			
#$1^3/_4$ page scenes			
#2+ page scenes			
Continue charting as in the multi-camera chart, following your characters, sets, etc.			

The Rule of Three

You have to read and analyze at least three scripts to make your chart effective. Why three? Because comedy has a rule of three? Because three's my lucky number? Because there are three Stooges? All true, but none is the reason you need to read three scripts. The number three forms a pattern, and patterns are what you are looking for.

If you only have one script as a model, you run the risk of merely imitating the style. You don't want to blindly copy an exact number. That will limit your creativity. Your script may be correct, but it will have a predictable feel. It will be okay, but an okay script is not what gets you an interview. Remember the Big Pile of Okay.

Having two scripts to compare is certainly better than reading just one, but you won't get the range you need to write an authentic episode of that show and still have the freedom to be original while staying within the form. Get three.

Finding the Range

After you fill in your chart, you can begin to get to know your show from the inside out. By discovering the patterns, you will develop instincts for your show. Knowing how many times a character appears or how many sets a show uses are important factors in determining how you tell your story. If you notice that a supporting character appears in two scenes in one of your samples and only one scene in the others, you've got a good indicator that you shouldn't overinvolve this character in your plotline. You may discover that this show's scenes run shorter as they build to the Act Break. You may find there is always a long scene near the end where the lead cop lays out how the perp did the crime and explains the motives.

Finding the *range* in each category will give you an instinct for how the show is structured, and the structure is what makes any television script, drama or comedy, work. Not the clever repartee (*Gilmore Girls*), not the pop soundtrack (*Cold Case*), not the catchphrases (*The Simpsons*) or character quirks (*Monk; Desperate Housewives*). These elements are fun and vitally important in any TV show, and you certainly don't want to leave them out of your script—but the real basis of successful series television is the story structure. Knowing how a show lays out on the page gives you the keys to structuring your story. Later I will show you more ways to use your chart to help with rewrites, but for now just get to know your show by the numbers.

Why Do I Need to Know This Stuff?

The counting and charting suggested in this chapter will not produce a story or even a story idea—we'll get to that in the next chapter—but they will give you strong indicators as to how to tell the story when you find one.

The numbers make the style and structure less mysterious and more accessible. Less magical and more doable.

If your spec script follows the prevailing patterns, it will read like the real thing. Your reader won't necessarily know why, but she will feel that you captured the show.

Do the writing staffs have to do this kind of breakdown? No. Because they are there every day. They are living and breathing the show and there's lots of support in the form of notes from and rewrites by the Executive Producer to keep them on track. They've internalized the show and have built-in instincts for it. By doing this kind of detailed analysis of your sample scripts, you are as close as you can get to the show without being on it.

However, if you do get a job on a show, as a new writer it would be a good idea to study the pilot and several episodes in this way. Get episodes written by the Executive Producer. The closer you get to his style, the more valuable you are going to be as a staff writer.

PART II

What You Need to Do

3. WHAT'S A STORY

Moving on! On shoot night of a TV sitcom, the audience and the staff, crew, and cast love to hear the A.D.* call out, "Moving on!" It means that the current scene has completed filming and we are "moving on" to the next scene. It is the sound of progress. It is the sound of one step closer to going home. It's a very good sound.

So here we are, *moving on* to another big step in the process of creating your spec script: choosing a story to write. It's not enough for a story to just be funny, scary, wild, crazy, or to have actually happened. A good story for a spec script must have these three (three again) specific elements.

Elements of a Spec Script Story

1. Your story must revolve around the Central Character
This may sound obvious to you, and I hope it does, but I make a point of this because I see so many spec scripts, and hear

---

*Assistant Director

so many ideas for spec script stories, that are not about the Central Character.

The Central Character is the one whose name is in the title of the show—*My Name Is Earl, Monk, Everybody Hates Chris,* or *Grey's Anatomy.* Sometimes it's not the name but the description of the character—for example, *Medium* or *Family Guy.*

If the name of the Central Character and the name of the actor playing the character are one and the same—*Everybody Loves Raymond, Reba, The Bernie Mac Show*—that's not just the Central Character, that's the show's STAR. When you have a star, it's even more imperative that your story revolve entirely around that character. Not necessarily for ego reasons, although that can certainly be a factor, but because the star is the engine of that show. The star is who the audience tunes in to see.*

What it means for a story to revolve around the Central Character is:

a) The story must have an emotional conflict for the Central Character.

b) The Central Character drives the action, that is, his choices make the plot progress.

c) The Central Character resolves the problem.

In other words, the story is told from the Central Character's point of view. It happens to him; and even more important, he makes it happen.

If your show has two characters in the title, such as *Two and a Half Men,* then you've got a buddy show, the classic of which was *The Odd Couple,* from which all buddy shows derive. Look over your

---

*Yes, all the actors in a TV show are stars, but they are the "starring in" kind of star, not The Star around whom the show was conceived.

research chart; you may determine that even though you have two leads, one of them drives the story more often than the other. For a spec script, it's probably a good idea to follow that pattern and tell a story that centers on the character the show uses more often. If the two leads are truly equal, then you get to pick which one will be the Central Character of your story, but you must involve the other lead almost as much. It's a buddy show. That's the franchise.

With a show like *Desperate Housewives* or *Entourage*, the title tells you that you have an ensemble show, meaning a group of characters that are equally important, or nearly so. In an ensemble show, episodes often revolve around a theme with story lines for the various characters. Using your research chart, determine how much story time each character gets. Even in ensemble shows, one character is usually slightly more prominent than others. If, for example, in a *Desperate Housewives* script, you choose to emphasize a Lynette story line, you'll want to make sure that Susan's story is also strong because she is the central character in that ensemble.

There are shows with no character name in the title, such as *CSI, Law & Order*, and *Without a Trace*. These are shows where the *procedure* is primary. The genre is even referred to as "procedurals." However, they still have Central Characters. Look at your research chart. Which character is in the most scenes and how many? Which character solves the case? Is it the same in every episode? If these factors shift to different characters in different episodes, you have a choice of which character to feature in your script. Be careful on these shows, because even though guest characters may figure prominently, your regular character will still be the Central Character and you should structure your story line accordingly.

The character with the most power is not necessarily the Central Character. The Central Character is the one who has the biggest struggle. On *Raymond*, for example, Marie had the most power, but she was never the Central Character. On *Scrubs*, the doctors, the nurses, and even the janitor, have more power than JD, but he is the Central Character.

Identify your Central Character and create your story, whatever it is, around that character.

2. Your story must use all of the regular supporting characters

The regular characters are the ones featured in the opening credits. They appear in every episode, and therefore, they all must be in your spec script. When thinking of possible story ideas, be aware that unless your Central Character has a conflict that involves a regular character, you don't have a workable idea for this show. Rule out ideas that create solitary confinement, lost at sea, home alone kinds of problems.

Characters who appear frequently or occasionally (depending on how many episodes the actor's contract calls for) are not regulars; they are recurring characters and their credit will appear at the end of each show they are in. It's fine to use a recurring character in your spec script, but you don't have to.

3. Your story must respect the premise of the show

This means that if, for example, your show is about a married man whose parents live across the street, you don't choose a story for your spec script in which he files for divorce or moves to Vancouver. Create a story that illustrates the basic elements of the show as they exist in the premise. Violating that principle is referred to as "testing the premise," and you want to avoid it when you're writing a spec.*

---

*Sometimes the staff will do a show that tests the premise. When a show does this, it's a good bet that it will be the show's last season. *Mad About You* did it when Jamie had the baby. The show was no longer about a young married couple hot for each other and keeping romance alive, it was about

Your spec script is not an opportunity to demonstrate how much better the show would be if it were different. Your spec script is your opportunity to demonstrate how close you can come to exactly what the show is about and still be original—which, incidentally, is a much more difficult task.

Stories to Avoid

Introducing an outside character

This is the single most frequent mistake I see in spec scripts. Writers may think they're showing how original they are, but what they are really showing is that they aren't excited enough by the show. I've said this before, but it is so important it bears repeating: Your spec script MUST revolve around the established Central Character and the other regular characters of the show.

If you introduce a significant new character, you are seriously diminishing the value of your spec script, the purpose of which is to show that you can write what somebody else wants written; that you can color inside the lines and still make it fresh. In other (very important) words, that you can write for hire! And isn't that the point?

If you are in love with a story idea that you think needs an outside character, see if you can reinterpret the story to work for one of the regular characters instead of an entirely new one. For example, I was working with a client who wanted to do a *Two and a Half Men* spec about Charlie meeting an unattractive girl whom he likes a lot as a friend, but doesn't want to date or sleep with.

_____

a married couple settling down with a baby and it was off the air the following year. That may not have been the only reason, but it certainly contributed.

The story, as my client conceived it, involved the girl trying to seduce Charlie, being rejected, getting mad, telling Charlie off . . . It was all about the girl. Sure, Charlie was involved, but the outside character had the problem and she was the one driving the story. All Charlie could do was back away.

Not a promising story for a spec, but there was a good idea in there and one my client had a personal stake in. So we looked at the emotional core of the idea and discovered that the basic idea was about dating insecurity. Once she realized that, it was easy for her to turn it into a story for Alan (the Jon Cryer character) instead of the outside character. She used Alan's dating fear and made him the one who wants to add sex to a relationship with a woman who doesn't think of him "in that way."

Now she had potential to involve the regulars in meaningful ways. Alan could learn from Charlie how to be sexier, more daring, and less vulnerable. Alan's son might poke holes in Alan's new persona, exposing his insecurities. Alan could stand up for himself and tell the woman off, and thus, in an ironic twist, make himself more attractive to her.

Yes, there's still a guest character involved, but she is not driving the story—Alan is. It would be possible to do the whole episode with the woman appearing in only one scene, which would be an acceptable use of an outside character.

BIG EXCEPTION: If you are doing a show where the basic premise requires guest characters every week—medical shows have new patients, cop shows have new criminals and victims—then, yes, the template of the show requires new characters. Therefore, you create new characters, but you must be especially careful that those characters do not take over the story. The emotional core and plot still must be carried by the regular cast.

A famous guest star

It's called *stunt casting* and I know many shows do it, but it should be avoided in your spec script; it says you're more interested in casting than in writing.

I've written a few episodes for guest stars myself, because the show already had the star lined up and needed a story. When I was on staff of *A Whole New Ballgame*—a series that lasted from 1995 to a little later in 1995—I wrote an episode of the show that featured the heavyweight champion Joe Frazier as himself. He was very nervous about acting in the show and being in front of a live audience. We did several takes and when it was over I asked Joe how he felt. He gripped my arm—oh yes, it was a powerful grip—and said, "I'd rather fight George Foreman than do that scene again." I didn't ask if he was referring to my writing or his acting.

The past lover

Please, don't write this as your spec script, especially if the ex-boy/girlfriend returns in a quirky, unexpected way. It seems like every third spec script I read is a version of this story. Could you turn this idea into a story for your regulars? Maybe if your character runs into the old lover off-screen and the story is actually about the repercussions between your Central Character and his or her current significant other. Still, it's such an overused idea I say tank this one. You can do better.

Aliens

Do not have aliens land in the backyard, infiltrate the office heating ducts, or kidnap the children. Unless your show is firmly situated in the sci-fi genre and already has folks from other planets on it, do not introduce an alien to your cast of characters.

The class reunion show

A bad choice for so many reasons. Besides being a much-used premise, which is reason enough to avoid it, anything involving the past history of your characters is shaky territory for a spec script. You will be inventing backstory about the characters, which is overstepping for a spec script. It's really only appropriate for the show's creator to invent backstory, so leave the reunion show to him or her. When a show actually does one of these (and almost all do some version of this), it kind of says "we're out of new ideas this week, so we're doing the class reunion show." That may be fine for writers who already have a job, but it is certainly not the message you want your spec to deliver.

Trading places

This one I call "Ricky in the Kitchen," as in the classic *I Love Lucy* episode where Ricky tries to do Lucy's job—pots overflow, the oven explodes, smoke billows—it was great when they did it in 1954, and it's still fun on TVLand, but I suggest you stay away from stories where the leads exchange roles. They can come across as contrived and gimmicky.

Trapped in an elevator/mountain cabin/bathroom/ wherever

Dick Van Dyke got caught in a cabin in the snow and every sitcom since has done some version of this story line. The underground parking garage episode on *Seinfeld* was a pretty brilliant take on this old plot. If you've got something that fresh, okay—otherwise, come up with another idea.

More Things to Stay Away From

Animals and babies

Avoid using them unless you're writing animation, or your show has an established animal on it (such as Eddy on *Frasier*). Same thing goes for babies. Keep their use to a minimum and never focus your episode around them. Why? Well, animals and babies don't talk, so there goes your sparkling dialogue. (Or if they do, the show usually bombs. I know firsthand; I was on the staff of *Baby Talk*.) Plus, any producer will see red flags. Animals and babies are hard to work with, they're unpredictable, there are restrictions on working hours, there are parents and trainers to deal with—just too many special needs. Even though they aren't going to shoot your spec script, you want to show that you know the boundaries; you'll look ready for professional consideration.

Flashbacks/fantasies/dream sequences

These devices usually betray weakness in your storytelling craft. If you're thinking of using these tricks, I strongly urge you to reconceive your story without them. It may be hard to figure out, but your script will be stronger for it. The exception, of course, is if flashbacks or dream sequences are an integral part of the show, like they are on *Without a Trace, Lost,* or *Medium.* Then, of course, you must use them.

If your show does use flashbacks or dream sequences, chart them explicitly: how often, who has them, how long are they.

Figure out what purpose they serve in telling the story. Even though they take place in the past, you must use them in ways that move your story forward. On *Medium* they're often used to illuminate Allison's fear. On *Without a Trace* they frequently illustrate character motives that aren't apparent in the simple facts of the case.

Elaborate sets/exotic locations

Don't take your characters camping, send them to Paris, or put them on a cruise ship. Not in a spec script. Those episodes are reserved for hit shows in their seventh season when the Executive Producer has earned a perk.

Follow your chart to see what the regular locations and sets are. Set limitations are part of episodic television. When you produce a show a week, you've got to use the regular sets for most of the scenes. There isn't time to build a bunch of new sets, there isn't space on the sound stage for them, and there isn't money in the budget. Again, respecting limits shows you understand the series business.

There's an emotional aspect to using the same sets as well. In a TV series, familiarity does not breed contempt, it breeds comfort. The audience wants to see the same characters in the same place again and again. Repetition is the lifeblood of series television. Embrace the familiar, and then make it fresh.

Pop culture references

Trendy references turn into clichés fast and, more important, leaning on a familiar name or product to get an easy laugh feels cheap. It might be okay to resort to shortcuts if you're on staff and have to get out a new script every week, but this is your very special spec script, the one that's going to open doors. It's got to be better.

Resist the temptation to do jokes on Viagra, BOTOX, breast

implants, or whatever current references are earning frequent flyer miles in the late-night talk show monologues. This is where you have to sense the line. There's a big difference between familiar and predictable. Familiar is comfortable; predictable is tired and derivative. You do not want those words on the coverage report for your script.

A word about product placement here. More and more shows are being required by the networks to include specific products in their content, but I don't think you need to do it for your spec script. It's a reality in the marketplace, but there's a lot of controversy about it from the creative community. I don't think any showrunner feels great about doing it and I don't think anyone wants to see it in a spec script. I think it's an issue you deal with when you are actually on a show and it's demanded of you.

4. FINDING YOUR STORY

So what can you do if everything that's been done can't be done? What else is there?

There's you. And that's where you go for stories. You must find stories that have something about them that is emotionally meaningful to you (that's your original voice), and then transfer that passion to the established character in the world of his or her show (and there's the form). In order to bring your personal connection to a story, you need to find out why you want to tell that story.

Selling vs. Telling

We know why you want to sell your story ($), but more important, why do you want to tell it? Why you want to tell it is where "you" are in the story. What makes a story original is not the theme—there are only so many themes, so they're going to be in constant circulation—but the specific way you choose to illustrate your theme. That comes from you, your observations and your life.

I was consulting with a writer who had a pitch meeting coming up for *Desperate Housewives.* She was thinking of pitching a story about Susan's daughter trying out for the cheerleading squad. When I asked her why she wanted to tell this story, she said, "Because it's about cheerleaders and cheerleaders are sexy. If I pitch a story with sexy girls, they may buy it."

That's a marketing researcher's reason, not a writer's reason. It's not a writer's reason because there's no emotional core; where are you going to go for the story? Short skirts? That's wardrobe, not story. Tryouts with a lot of girls jumping around in short skirts? That's a scene, maybe a good one, but remember, the story must revolve around the Central Character. What's Susan's story?

After some probing we got to the real reason, a writer's reason: "I want to do a story about Susan's daughter trying out for cheerleading because when I was in high school I wanted to be a cheerleader, but I was too scared to go out for it because I wasn't popular. I was fat, had bad skin, and was uncoordinated." The important words are "I was too scared." Fear drives a character, and this particular fear had personal meaning for the writer. That's a connection to a story. That's why you want to tell it.

Now the writer had a story about Susan pushing her daughter into cheerleading, because Susan had missed the opportunity when she was young. The showrunner would be able to imagine the scene with cute girls in short skirts, so she's included her sexy selling point, but the story idea clearly revolves around an emotional issue for Susan and the inherent conflict between her and her daughter.

A Personal Personal Connection

Everybody Loves Raymond was a show about family relationships, particularly how your parents can still complicate your life even when you're an adult. So when I was a Co-Executive Producer on staff and was thinking about stories to do, I looked at my own relationship with my parents. Here's how I came up with the story for the *Everybody Loves Raymond* episode "You Bet," the one where Ray discovers that Frank has been using him to up his betting odds.

When I was a kid growing up in Sioux City, Iowa, my dad owned a jewelry store where he sold Speidel watchbands and Sunbeam toasters to corn and soybean farmers. He just loved everything about being a businessman. I, on the other hand, was an artist, but my dad didn't seem to recognize my talents or take any particular interest in them. Until one day, when he presented me with a proposal: Since I was so "artistic," I should come down to his store and decorate the display windows.

He thought this was a great idea, but to me it was like being punched in the stomach. I felt like the only way my father could relate to me, or see any value in me or my talent, was if it was "useful" for his business.

Maybe that was an immature teenager's self-centered reaction, but I still get upset thinking about it, and that's good enough for a story idea. (Also a good reason to go to therapy, but maybe not until after I'd gotten a story out of it.)

I connected with that emotional current and then translated it into the characters of Ray and Frank in the world of the show. Ray's character on the show worked as a sportswriter. His dad paid no attention to his writing, but in "You Bet," Frank shows sudden and uncharacteristic interest and appreciation for Ray's work. At first, Ray feels gratified, respected even, but when Ray discovers that his father has been using him to get inside information to improve his betting odds, those feelings turn to feelings of betrayal, disappointment, and anger.

This gave me a strong emotional narrative and a script that I really wanted to write. Even though "You Bet" has no actual details of my life, the concept came from my connection to the emotional issue.

You are writing from personal experience, but you are not writing a personal memoir when you write for TV. You don't need to use all the external details for your story. You can, but it's the emotional content you want. That is what connects you personally to a story. It's why you care. That's crucial, because unless you care, deeply, the story will lack passion.

Without passion, your script may be competent, credible, and correct, but it will not jump up off the page and excite somebody about your writing. Only passion will do that. That's not to say your script doesn't need to be competent, credible, and correct—it does, absolutely. It has to be all that *and* have passion to get the attention of someone who might want to pay you to write.

Good stories come from emotional issues: fear, anger, secret desires. But these are general emotions and it can be hard to find a specific story from such a large arena, so I've got an exercise that I like to use to break these big emotions down and enable you to get connected in a tangible way.

Exercise—Where Do You Get Your Ideas?

You know the Seven Deadly Sins? I consider them story gold mines. Pick a sin, any sin. (In case the only sin you can remember is Lust, there's a list on my example pages later in this chapter.) Your favorite, your least favorite, it doesn't matter which one; they all lead to human failings, which is the best place for stories to come from.

If you have no story ideas yet, this exercise will help you find some. If you have an idea but not a powerful emotional connection to it yet, use this exercise to get to your emotions.

Write the sin you picked at the top of a piece of paper. Now write down a number of instances when you have been guilty of that sin. Keep in mind that you are looking for things you're *guilty* about. For example, if you pick Pride, it's not about finding things you are rightfully proud of, it's about the *sin* of Pride—when you were too proud to admit you were wrong, or too proud to admit you needed help. The woman in the preceding example—the one who was afraid to try out for cheerleading—could use the sin of Pride. Perhaps her fear made her too proud to risk failing.

You're looking for the embarrassing and humiliating times. Be honest and you'll turn up better material. Use shorthand—don't write a whole page of anecdotal narrative, just a few words that identify the guilt for you. The examples don't have to be profound, important, or dramatic. It's actually better if they're not. What's important is that they be from your life and that they be *specific*.

Writing something general that you think you would be guilty of or that you are often guilty of will not give you the emotional material that an actual specific instance will. If you chose Wrath as your sin and you write down "when people cut in front of me in traffic," you will not get as close to your emotional connection as you will if you write down "Blue Mercedes convertible cut in front of me on Pacific Coast Highway." Or if you pick Sloth and write "avoiding paying bills," that's general. But if you identify a specific time that you avoided paying bills and watched the *Family Guy* marathon instead, you've got a concrete experience and that will work a lot better for the exercise.

Look at the following examples. Each one is a specific thing I actually did at a specific moment.

THE SEVEN DEADLY SINS, AKA STORY GOLD MINES

LUST   WRATH   PRIDE   ENVY   GREED   (GLUTTONY)   SLOTH

Eating a pound of salted Trader Joe peanuts until I'm sick

Eating an entire Sara Lee brownie cake

Eating all the leftover salmon, not leaving any for my husband

Eating 25 artichoke hearts at Melissa's wedding buffet

Swiping my cousin Sharon's piece of cake off her plate when she wasn't looking

Licking salad dressing off my plate

Eating shoestring potatoes constantly for four hours at a taping of The Mommies *because they were free and they were there*

Ordering all the desserts on the menu at an expense account lunch with Leo

Refusing to split an Italian chocolate ice cream bombe with my daughter at Bruno's

Making 3 dozen chocolate chip cookies and eating them all before my kids got home

Now you.

Give yourself a short time limit. Two minutes works for me. This will spur you to come up with examples spontaneously, and will help you resist the temptation to go on and on describing one event. Use a timer so you won't have to take yourself out of the exercise to check the clock. Use the microwave timer if your writing area is close to the kitchen—whose isn't?

Pick a sin, set your timer, and Do It.

Exercise—Cluster

The next step is to do a cluster. I didn't make this one up; almost every creative writing teacher uses variations of this exercise. I learned it in a writing class with Nan Hunt, a poet who taught an approach to writing influenced by Jungian psychology. Couldn't be further from TV writing. But I find it invaluable for getting under my linear-thinking brain to a more gut level of exploration, and so I've adapted it for use as the next part of the Seven Sins Exercise. I find it a great resource for discovering inciting incidents, illuminating unique character moments, or even finding a whole story theme.

You've got some specific personal stuff in your list under your chosen sin. Pick the most embarrassing one. It's okay, no one will know it's you once you get through with this exercise.

Find an image—make sure it's just an image, not a run-on sentence describing the incident. In the example I've done to illustrate this exercise, I picked the time I ate an entire Sara Lee brownie cake, slice by thin slice, without even waiting for it to defrost, not saving a single crumb for any loved ones—but I didn't use the whole story as my center. I used only the image that symbolized that incident—the brownie cake—to set up my exercise.

Find your symbol image and write it in the middle of the page. Then circle it. I like to circle it because a) it focuses me and b) it keeps my pen on the page, which is a great technique for keeping linear thinking at bay. As long as your pen is moving, you are exploring. As soon as it stops, you are thinking. Danger zone! With thinking comes analyzing, judging, and criticizing. Right now you want to be free of all that, and the more your pen is moving, the freer you'll be.

So now, cluster around the image, writing down sensory associations and imagery. Draw lines like spokes reaching out, keeping you connected to the center image and also—so important—your pen on the page. Work from the center out, all over the page. You're not making a list. You're tapping into your life, which is not a tidy, logical process. I find writing all over the page keeps my dreaded self-editor confused enough to be quiet.

And write fast. This is not about thinking up the right answers, it's about discovery, surprise, and spontaneity.

The exercise will be most useful to you as a tool if you stay with imagery that connects with your senses. Colors you saw, the texture on your fingertips, heat you felt on the back of your neck, the smell in the air, sounds that you heard—not just the radio, but what voice on the radio, what song, what part of the song. The more specific you can be about it, the better.

But don't write down how you feel about the song. Write down how things feel in your body, or on your skin, but not how they feel emotionally. When you write what you feel emotionally, it's actually coming from your analytical mind. Trust the concrete imagery to connect you with your emotional life without describing your emotional life.

It's surprisingly hard to stay on the simple sensory images. I do this exercise in many of the classes I teach, and when we go over them, it usually takes three or four attempts for the writers to go for just what they see, hear, smell, taste, and feel with their body. The natural inclination is to describe, evaluate, and comment on the memory rather than to simply enter it and reexperience it through the senses. Avoid the narrative or judgmental—those come from your conscious mind and that horrible inner editor we're avoiding.

Stay within the discipline of the sensory connection, because that is where the value of the exercise lies. Let your free association happen in random ways, rather than making deliberate connections or any kind of narrative sense.

We'll want your narrative head later when it's time to structure your story. We're even going to want that annoying self-editor who evaluates, judges, and criticizes, but not until much later. Right now allow yourself to indulge in discovery for its own sake.

Here is my example:

Klimt poster

white ball

bare feet on smooth wood floor

those colored

awkward word chewy

beige cork top

nubby fabric

creamy smooth

thick choc goo on joint

roof of mouth

choc smell

takes bus trip ban off baseball game

chocolate fingers

licks

licking inside of tin

tin against tongue

l against teeth

choc between teeth

silver underside

yellow

peel back kurls

BROWNIE

TV sounds

"you sittin'"

Garret / Trudi

sick stomache

laughs

sister's boyfriend

bad red sofa

scratchy on backs of thighs

silver knife

slices

silver tin

cardboard cover

into mouth

thin slice

again

again

another thin slice

smooth frosting on tongue

l paper thin slice

Your turn. Give yourself two or three minutes on the timer. Your mind is less likely to wander and start editing when you know you only have to stay with it for a brief time. Don't worry about doing it right, just give it a try.

Mining the Cluster

Now that you've done the cluster exercise—you did do it, didn't you? You didn't just think about it? Writing is putting words on paper. If it's in your head, you're thinking, you may even be thinking about writing, but you're not writing.

So now that you've done the cluster, what do you do with what you found? Allow what you've discovered to spark your story by transferring it to a character. Here's an example of how I might use my experience of the Sara Lee brownie binge in a hypothetical story for *Everybody Loves Raymond.*

I translate this guilty pleasure of eating something forbidden to the character of Debra. I start with an image that emerged when I did my cluster. The image of "licking the inside of the tin" strikes me and I build out from that. I ask myself questions like, "What circumstance would get Debra to the point of licking the last bit of fudge frosting out of a frozen cake pan?" Well, maybe she's supposed to be on a diet. She'd be embarrassed if she got caught. If this is going to be an *ELR* story, I want to get Ray into the action, so I want it to be most embarrassing if Ray catches her. How can I do that? What if I set up a challenge? Ray claims golf is as important to him as food is to her. Debra scoffs. To prove it, Ray challenges her—he will give up golf this weekend if she gives up sweets for one day.

Then I think more about Debra's circumstances—she's a mom, she's not a good cook. Then I think, I'm a mom, I'm a good cook, but

I don't have a lot of time to cook and I remember when I felt pressured to make something for the Halloween bake sale at my kid's school. So what if Debra commits to baking cookies for a school bake sale but she ruins them and ... here's what I came up with:

Debra's baking cookies for the kids' school while on a diet. Ray stuffs raw cookie dough in his mouth and makes fun of Debra. He predicts she'll never be able to stay away from sweets. Later, the cookies come out rock hard. Debra's too proud to ask Marie for help; instead, she gets a tin of Sara Lee brownies from the freezer to replace the bad cookies. She ignores the brownies, but she's drawn to them. They aren't even defrosted yet when she cuts a very thin slice out of the tin and savors it. It is heaven. She cuts another very thin slice. Then another. Less savoring, more gobbling this time.

Ray catches Debra running her finger along the inside of the now-empty Sara Lee brownie tin and licking the chocolate off it. She gives up on the finger and licks the pan. Ray watches her until Debra realizes she's not alone and Ray wins the challenge.

I used my own guilty experience to create a revealing moment for a character. If I hadn't done the exercise to discover my own real experiences with gluttony, I probably wouldn't have come up with this idea for a story. But even if I did, I might have used some standard cliché of emotional overeating, like having Ray catch Debra eating ice cream out of a container. That's okay, but dull; you've seen it too many times before.

This is fresher. The specifics I found in the cluster exercise will give my eventual scene more texture and action than a generic, Debra-eating-ice-cream scene could have. Working off this one image, I discovered a number of possible story beats. The setup—the Ray/Debra challenge. There's a possible earlier story beat implied, where Marie offers to make something for the bake sale and Debra takes up the challenge, insisting on doing it herself, and then doesn't want to admit failure.

It isn't autobiographical, it doesn't come out of the same circumstances as my incident, but it's my experience translated into the lives of my characters. It is this kind of authenticity that will give your script the fresh, original quality everyone is looking for. And you can't get it by making stuff up in your head—at least I can't. You've got to go through your gut.

So now you know where stories come from. Not from old TV shows, but from your own human failings. One of the great things about being a writer is that you can put your worst self to productive use. Your most humiliating experiences, your deepest fears, your most embarrassing longings, actually have value.

If you read a news article or hear a funny anecdote about a friend that you think might make a good story, or if you are assigned a story idea (write a great spec script and it'll happen), you can use the Seven Sins Exercise to get a personal connection. Pick the sin that you think might be operating in the story you read or heard or were assigned, and then tap into your own exploration of the emotional core.

Discover times when you were guilty of that sin and follow through with the cluster exercise. You will find a much more interesting and personally meaningful way into the story that first inspired you. You will find your passion for the story.

That is one way to get your personal creativity inside the form. If you do that, you are well on your way to writing an original story that shows you have imagination and still know how to serve the needs of the show. That's on the money! $20,956 for a half hour, $30,823 for an hour.* Now tell me that's not why you want to write for TV.

---

*According to the Writers Guild of America's 2006 Schedule of Minimums. And then there are the residuals! Love the MIMs (Money in the Mail).

5. THEME/PLOT

What's the Difference?

The theme is the central conflict in your story. It's what the story is *about.* You must identify your theme. It will be your single most important tool in the crafting of your story. An important note: What it's *about* is NOT what *happens.* You know how when somebody starts raving about a movie they just saw, and when you ask what it's about, they start with the opening and proceed to tell you everything that happened scene by scene? Boring, isn't it? Don't you just want them to stop? That's because what happens is the plot—but it's not what it's *about.*

What it's about is the emotional issue—the theme. Plot and theme are connected—at least they better be—but they are not the same. The plot (what happens) is the unique way you have chosen to illustrate the theme (what it's about).

For example: *Romeo and Juliet* is *about* love—young, passionate, forbidden love—versus family. What happens—well, you know what happens—boy meets girl, they fall in love, they kill themselves. That's the plot. It happens as a consequence of the theme, love vs. family honor.

So if everything that happens in a story is a consequence of what it's about, you can see why it is crucial to identify what it's about before you get very far. It can be difficult to do that; sometimes you have to noodle around with what you think might be happening in the plot to get clues as to what it's really about.

Let's look at "You Bet" again. I began with a single circumstance that I knew would be a part of a sportswriter's life. I figured that Ray would occasionally have information about an athlete's private life that could affect his performance on the field. That might be an ethical issue for Ray; should he use what he knows to place a bet? But that's not enough to tell me what it's about yet. It doesn't have any emotional connections for me, and it doesn't meet the three requirements of any episode.

It does meet the first one: it revolves around my Central Character, Ray. But it misses on the second requirement, as it doesn't involve any of my other regular characters; in fact, it threatens to involve an outside character, the athlete. It also doesn't meet the third requirement: respect the premise of the series, which on *Raymond* is: how do you manage to be a grown-up when your parents live across the street? Every episode of *Raymond* looks at that question. If it doesn't do that in some way, it isn't an *Everybody Loves Raymond* episode, or at least not a very good one.

Obviously I had to keep working on this idea before it could be a *Raymond* story. It wasn't until I got the issue off the athlete and connected it to Frank that I found out what the episode was going to be about—a son discovering that his father is using him for his own gain. As you know from the earlier discussion, that came from my own relationship with my father. Now it could be an *ELR* story and it had an emotional current that connected with me.

I might have told the story using Robert as Ray's opponent, but then it would have been a brothers' competition story, which would have worked but wouldn't have had as much personal meaning for me. If I hung the story only on Ray, without getting another member of the family involved in opposition, it would not be dynamic and it wouldn't serve the overall premise of the show.

Premise Line—the Essential Guide to Every Choice

Once you've found a theme, you need to turn that theme into a story premise that you can state in a single sentence. Your Premise Line is where your theme (what it's about) and your plot (what happens) meet. You don't need to state your theme outright in your Premise Line, but it should be implied.

You may hear people use the term log line interchangeably with premise line, but I like to make a distinction. I think of a log line as a marketing tool, something that would appear in the *TV Guide* listing to get you to watch the show. It doesn't reveal too much or give away the plot. It's just clever and fun and meant to tease you into seeing the show.

The Premise Line is not a marketing device; it's a working tool—for you. It's a line that lays out your story in a clear, concise way. You need it to be simple and short, because you will be referring to it constantly as a guide to your story development process.

I discovered how important a Premise Line is when I was working on *Raymond*. Every story was subject to network and studio approval before we could go forward in developing the script. We would send in what we called "2-pagers," treatments that described the narrative line of the prospective story in less than, that's right, two pages. Then Phil Rosenthal (the Executive Producer) and the Co-Executive Producers, of which I was one, would gather in Phil's office and listen to the speakerphone as the executives gave notes.

They seemed to have so many notes on every story. They were always confused; they just could not see the story. We would get a million questions and almost as many "solutions" (much worse than questions). This was frustrating; *we* knew the stories made sense, we could see how they would work. Why couldn't the execs?

After a few of these sessions, I suggested to Phil that we put a Premise Line at the top of the 2-pagers to serve as an intro to the story line they were about to read. Like in a classical Greek drama, the Chorus comes out onstage and tells you everything you're going to see and then Oedipus or Creon or whoever comes out and plays it. (Yes, I was a theater major in college.)

So we did that—we wrote a Premise Line and put it in bold at the top of the next 2-pager that went in. As if by magic, the questions stopped. The notes were simpler. A couple of the execs actually commented on how much better the story was that week. We put a Premise Line at the top of every 2-pager that went in for approval thereafter, and those speakerphone meetings went from 45 minutes down to 5.

The stories themselves weren't presented any differently, but once the execs were able to see the whole concept quickly, they could then read the story treatment and understand how each piece related to the others. The story made more sense, because they knew what it was about from the beginning.

You should have this advantage too. Do a Premise Line, even though you don't have executives scrutinizing your every move. It's surprisingly hard to summarize your story in one line, but keep at it. Get it simple, get it comprehensive. It will focus your story in a way that nothing else will, and it will make everything that comes after stronger, and maybe even easier to write.

As you develop your story and learn more about it, you may discover that what you are writing about has shifted. That's okay. That's development. Go back and adjust your Premise Line to reflect your changing story.

Elements of a Premise Line

There are three (three again!) basic elements that will guide you in coming up with your Premise Line.

1. Setup of a conflict

2. Turning point in the conflict

3. Confrontation or consequence as a result of the conflict

There's no set way for how a Premise Line should read, but here is a one-sentence template that can help you block out the basics.

TOOL BOX

> When (something happens), the Central Character (does something), which involves (other regular character) and then (something unexpected happens) because of it.

When something happens, that's your *setup;* when the lead character does something that involves another regular character and implies a conflict, that's your *turning point;* and when something happens because of it, that's your *confrontation/consequence.*

You can rephrase your line any way you want, but this will start you off with the basic elements that you want to cover.

Here's an example of a Premise Line for "The Invasion," an episode I wrote for *Everybody Loves Raymond* following the above template.

[The setup:] When the house needs fumigating, *[the turning point with implied conflict:]* Ray and Debra and the kids move in to Marie and Frank's house which *[the confrontation/consequence:]* gives Ray and Debra the chance to show Marie and Frank what it's like to have intrusive family members in your home.

In one line I get the idea of what the show is *about*—imposing on your family—and what *happens,* Ray and Debra move in with Marie and Frank because their house is being fumigated. Ray is driving the action, the other important characters are organically involved (even Robert is implied because he was living with his parents at that point), and the premise of the series—an adult still struggling to resolve parental issues—is served.

It's simple, and that's what's useful about it, but not easy! Give yourself some help.

Exercise—Warm-up for Premise Line

Every scene of the script will be built off of this Premise Line. As hard as it can be to formulate this line, it's worth the effort because it pays you back in so many ways as you develop your story.

Before attempting to write the Premise Line for your own story, write a Premise Line for one (or all three if you're ambitious) of the scripts that you've been analyzing. It's easier to do for someone else's finished script than for your own struggling-to-be-born one. Think of it as a warm-up.

If you've watched a baseball game, you've seen a hitter swing two bats at once, to warm up before coming to the plate. When he's up, his single bat will feel lighter, it will move easier and faster, and he'll swing with more power. More knowledgeable people than I have said that hitting a baseball is the most difficult thing in sports. I think creating a story that works ranks right up there on the writer's degree-of-difficulty scale, so if a professional ballplayer needs practice swings, why wouldn't you?

There's yet another reason why you need a Premise Line. When people ask you what you're working on, you want to be able to tell them in one simple, confident sentence. If you start to tell someone about what you're working on and you're unsure of it—since it isn't finished, how sure can you be?—you will lose confidence with each weakening word. If you're anything like me, your story will limp along as you struggle to make it sound fun and interesting.

But if you have your simple, short Premise Line, when someone casually asks what you're working on, it will fall easily from your lips. Your friend gets the idea immediately, smiles encouragingly (yes!), and you feel confident. Most important, you *appear* confident. If you're in Hollywood or anywhere nearby, appearance is all you need. Appear confident, and you *are* confident.

So, Premise Line: Get one.

6. SYNOPSIS

If you've got a working Premise Line, then you also have some elements of your plot. Great. We're moving on!

The synopsis* is a brief narrative of your story. It runs about half a page (single spaced) for a half-hour show, a page for a one-hour show. Again, don't squeeze or stretch your margins. The limited length is a tool, a guide to the kind of simplicity you want to strive for at this stage. You don't know all of your story, but you know enough at this point to write a synopsis. Your synopsis should have more specific plot turns in it than your Premise Line. It should also have indications of character motives in it. What it should not have is a lot of details.

---

*In film development, the term *synopsis* is often used to mean a treatment or an outline and it is expected to be a longer, more detailed account of your story than I am describing here.

Specifics vs. Details

Time-out to discuss the difference between *specifics* and *details*. Details are small stuff—jokes, staging business, logistics—and they will clutter up your story if you use them now. Save the details for when you write your first draft, at which point you will really need them. Specifics are what clarify and anchor your story—that's what you're looking for.

I'll give you some examples using "The Invasion" story again. If I write:

```
Ray and Debra have to move out of their
house, so they go to Frank and Marie's.
```

It would be right, but it's so general that I haven't done enough to move my story process forward. I need to figure out some specifics that will give me more story to go on. Why do they have to move out?

So how about if I write:

```
Ray and Debra discover that their house has
termites, so they have to move out for three
days while the exterminators fumigate.
```

Termites, moving out, three days, exterminators, fumigate—those are story *specifics*. They are building blocks for the framework of my story.

Let's compare creating a story to building a house. The first line, the too-general one, is like digging the hole for the foundation. The second one is like laying down a foundation beam.

But look what happens if I put in too many *details:*

```
Ray discovers a little pile of sawdust near
the door. He shows it to Frank, who recog-
nizes it as evidence of termites. Debra
```

```
wants Ray to call an exterminator, but he's
lazy and puts it off, so she has to do it.
```

None of that's wrong, but none of it belongs in a synopsis either. It's too detailed. This is how the page limit helps you. I'm not going to get to the big story points if I take the time and space to cover all these details. If we go back to the house analogy, I'm putting up wallpaper and moving in a sofa before there's a floor to put it on.

However, as you will have undoubtedly experienced, writing a story is not a neat and tidy process. Writing is an unruly affair, and the steps don't necessarily proceed with linear logic. I think of writing like a Möbius strip, a loop that twists around and feeds back on itself.

There is no beginning, no ending. The process is fluid and cumulative. Anything leads to everything.

So sometimes you need to dream about the wallpaper (and furniture) to figure out what size and shape the room is going to be. You're going to imagine details; just don't use them as story points, they're too weak. Find the support beams and build the structure of your story with those.

Warm-up Exercise

Like you warmed up with the Premise Lines, write a synopsis of your research script(s). I suggest you set a time limit for this exercise so you don't get lost in it—five minutes is good. It's not about getting it perfect. It's about getting used to the idea of telling a story in simple, broad strokes.*

Now write a synopsis of your own story. That will take considerably more than five minutes.

---

7. TURNING IDEAS INTO STORIES

It is not the answer that enlightens, it's the question.
—EUGENE IONESCO, PLAYWRIGHT

Who's Driving?

You know by now it's got to be your Central Character. In order to get the Central Character in the driver's seat, you want three (of course) things:

1. You want the story to be the Central Character's problem.

2. You want the Central Character to be the one who has the most to lose or gain.

3. You want the Central Character to resolve the problem.

If it sounds simple, it's because it is. Simple is what you are going for. But as we also know, simple is not easy.

So I have tools. The way I turn an idea into a story is to ask a lot of questions. The questions aren't a test of how much I already know, they are used as tools to discover how to tell my story. The questions don't necessarily have answers, certainly not easy ones. If, at this stage in your story development, you have a lot of answers, it may mean you aren't asking the right questions or allowing the questions to provoke your thoughts. Here are some questions that I think are essential to putting up the structural beams of the house that is going to be your story.

TOOL BOX

> What does the Central Character want?
> Why does he care about it?
> Who's against it or in the way?
> What's the risk?
> What's the fear?
> What's different about your Central Character by the end?

Let's take these questions one by one and examine how to use them as discovery tools. To illustrate, I'll use the episode "No Fat" that I wrote for *Everybody Loves Raymond*.*

What Does the Central Character Want?

Tangible goals

Your character wants some big overall thing: to find love, to pursue justice, to achieve success, to keep his family together. The premise of your series is based on whatever universal thing your character wants, and, therefore, your character is going to

---

*If you'd like to see these examples in context, you can go to my website, www.SandlerInk.com, where you'll find the complete script for "No Fat." You'll also find my developmental notes, including my synopsis and two-page treatment and outline so you can track how the story evolved.

want that in some way every week. What you need to do for your spec script is identify a specific goal that illustrates that big want. It must be specific and it must be tangible.

Does it have to be? Yes, it has to be. The goal has to be something you can name, something that we can see when and if your character gets it.

In "No Fat," Ray's goal is to have a traditional Thanksgiving feast. A traditional meal arrives in a big cardboard box—the characters can touch it, see it, smell it, taste it. It can be seen on film. And finally, at the end of the story, Ray and the whole family sit around the table and eat it. It doesn't get more tangible than that.

. . . Not to be

Goals function best if they are active rather than static or passive. In other words, if you find yourself describing your character's goal as "to be" something—to be the best basketball player, to be a mother, to be in love—that is static. It's not wrong, but you can make that goal more active by making it specific: to win the state championship, to adopt a child. Romeo's goal is not "to be in love," his goal is to marry Juliet. Or if he's in a teen comedy: to get laid. Now your character is in active pursuit of something, and pursuit is what you need to drive a story.

Positive goals

State your character's drive as a positive, not a negative. If you've identified your character's objective as *not* to do something, change it around to reflect what it is that the character *does* want. You can't describe or show behavior that is *not* happening.

For instance, if you've identified your character's goal as "to not get caught by the police," visualize what that would look like. I can't see an image. But make it a positive action like "to hide from the police" or "to destroy the evidence" and images immediately come to my mind—crouching in a Dumpster, throwing stolen jewelry into a sewer. Now you've got action and something you can show.

Why Does Your Central Character Care About This Goal?

It's got to be important to your character. It doesn't have to be important to the world—often the more trivial the issue, the better the story—but you must create an emotional imperative that's believable for the character. *Seinfeld* perfected a character's obsession with the trivial.

When I was first developing the story for "No Fat," I didn't know it was going to be about Thanksgiving; I knew only Marie was going to change how she cooked and that was going to upset Ray. Once I found Thanksgiving (actually I didn't find it, it was given to me by Steve Skrovan, another writer on staff), the story began to take shape.

The main way Ray relates to his mom is through food, and so focusing the issue around Thanksgiving, where food plays a big role, and making it his favorite meal, heightens the importance for him.

Who's Against It or In the Way?

This is usually another character, an important regular. In "No Fat," Marie was in the way of Ray's getting his goal of a traditional Thanksgiving dinner and Debra supported her, so Ray had a lot of opposition. That gave me the structure for my story. I knew that the big moment of confrontation, the climax, would play out between Ray and Marie. I didn't know what the moment was yet, but I knew where to look for it.

What's the Risk?

The tangible plot risk is that Ray will lose out on his favorite meal. The emotional risk is that his mother will find out that he cares more about himself than about her. And who doesn't? That's what makes it relatable.

Ray gives in to his all-too-human nature, and we recognize ourselves in him. The audience will care because they know it's a true moment and that they might have done the same thing.

Knowing the emotional risk tells me the high point (or is it the low point?) in the script: when Ray gets caught. I didn't know how that was going to happen, but I knew that if I kept asking myself, "What is Ray risking?" I would come up with something that would work for the story. When I found it, that turned out to be my Act Break.

What's the Fear?

Facing his mom's emotions. Ray's afraid of feelings, his own or anyone else's. In this case it's especially hard for him, because it's his mom and he's guilty for hurting her. He's afraid to face her when she's upset. Connecting the Central Character's fear to the confrontation with the opponent provides good support for the story structure.

TURNING IDEAS INTO STORIES   77

What's Different About Your Central Character by the End?

It's a sitcom series, so not that much, but Ray has a moment where he sees his mom differently than he ever did before, even if it's only for just a moment. When he apologizes to her, he acknowledges that her needs are as valid as his own; he relates to his mom as a person, not just a mother. It's a mature moment for Ray and it's difficult for him, so while it's a small moment in the scheme of things, it's a big moment for Ray.

These are the structural beams that support a story. You won't know the answers right away, but if you've identified what you're looking for, you'll have a blueprint to guide your discovery process and you'll build a stronger story.

WARNING: Your logical brain is going to want to turn these guidelines into a formula. Please, resist the temptation. These questions are tools, not rules. They're more flexible than rules or formulas. They won't work the same way every time, but if you use them to explore your raw material, they will turn up surprising stuff.

8. THE PLOT THICKENS

Getting Set Up

The Setup is usually the easiest part of the story to come up with. Very often a writer will come up with a Setup and think that is the story. It's not. Your story is what happens *after* your Setup. That's why it's called a Setup; it sets up the story that is to come.

I have a special tool just for Setups. I call it *Mah Nish Tah Nah.* What?? Okay, bear with me.

If you're Jewish, maybe you recognize these as the opening words of the four questions asked by the youngest child at a traditional Passover Seder. For those of you who are not Jewish, and for those Jews who have forgotten whatever they might have known, I will translate: *Mah Nish Tah Nah* are the Hebrew words that begin the question "Why is tonight different from all other nights?"

From this question the entire biblical story of Exodus pours forth at the Passover Seder. It can take twenty-five minutes or four hours, and is always followed by a sumptuous meal. It's a pretty important question.

By asking this question in your story development process, you will markedly strengthen your Setup. Whatever your inciting incident is, ask, "Why today?" "What makes it different today?" It doesn't have to be profound. It can be a very little thing. You can create a story without doing this, but if you identify "why today" you will have deepened the core believability of your story and you will have galvanized the motivation behind your character's desire for achieving his goal. You will also find some good story beats.

If your Setup is that your character wants to get a dog, what's different about today? Did she want a dog yesterday? Why is today the day she's going to look for a dog? Because the neighbor's apartment was robbed last night? Because her boyfriend dumped her last night? Because her friend just got engaged to a guy she met at the dog park?

Find a reason that means something to your character and let that set your story in motion. If you invest the inciting incident with more heft, the emphasis will be on the emotional motives and you can turn a tired old idea like getting a dog into something fresh. She doesn't ever have to get the dog, because it's just a Setup for the real story: fear of being alone. That fear could be getting robbed, getting over a lost boyfriend, desperate/stupid attempts to meet a guy, or all of them.

TOOL BOX

Mah Nish Tah Nah, i.e., Why today? Ask this question to anchor your inciting incident.

Let the Character Lead You to the Plot

When I was a new mother, I went regularly to a group for parents with infants run by Magda Gerber, a Hungarian woman with a unique approach to child rearing. Her method was to let the child discover her world for herself. If the baby reaches for a toy, don't pick it up and hand it to her. Let her get it herself. She may struggle to get it, but she will learn to crawl and she will learn to get things for herself. The baby gets to have the satisfaction of accomplishment. You, the parent, witness the discovery process and delight in your child. This philosophy changed my whole relationship with my children, and, though I didn't realize it at the time, it also changed my relationship with my characters.

Don't plot the story for your character. Allow your character to reach for what he wants. Let him go after it himself. You follow, you witness, and write down what he does. Are you worried that nothing will happen if you don't make it happen?

Well, of course, you're making it happen, but by allowing your character to lead you instead of the other way around, you will be less manipulative. It's like a Ouija board. You put your hands on the pointer, another person puts her hands on the pointer and neither of you moves it, yet somehow it moves! It finds letters and spells out words.

Let your character be the other hand on the pointer. Rather than making your character do things, allow yourself to delight in your character as he surprises you, and if you do, chances are good that your reader will also be delighted.

Emotional Action

A good way to allow your character to lead is to discover plot points through emotional action. What makes a character do what she does? The motivations, the expectations, and the compensating behavior when things don't go as planned. You must be true to the character, yet find things that the character has not done before.

Pull from your own life experiences, not other movies or TV shows you've seen. Beware: sometimes it's hard to tell the difference. If, for example, your character is nervous about dating, you ask yourself, what do I do when I'm scared to ask a woman out on a date? Listen carefully to your answer. Are you describing what you *would* do? If so, that's general and probably based on what you've seen in movies and TV shows.

On the other hand, if you find yourself describing a specific time when you behaved in a certain way, like in the cluster exercise, you're connecting with real behavior. That's what you want. What you *really* do is always more interesting and original than what you think you *would* do.

Keep in mind that it's not enough for your character to feel something, no matter how deeply. Those feelings must make your character do something. Your job as a writer is to identify what your character feels and then to translate your character's feelings into actions. What your character does because of his emotion is what will convey to the audience what the character is feeling.

Uta Hagen, in her seminal book *Respect for Acting*, said this: "Acting is doing . . . everything should lead to action." She exhorts actors to ask themselves, "What do I do to get what I want? How do I get what I want? (By doing what?)" and "What do I do to overcome the obstacles, and how do I overcome them? (By doing what?) Look for active verbs!"

These are the very questions you, the writer, must ask when creating a story for your character.

Obstacles

Obstacles are what keeps the plot moving, and every dramatic writing theory talks about creating them. I prefer to call obstacles *consequences.* I think that by defining obstacles as consequences you can better understand how they are directly connected to your character's action and, therefore, you will create genuine plot escalation.

When I consult with writers on their stories, I will often see that they have made up obstacles which do not make the story escalate. They just repeat the same obstacle over and over with different circumstances or props. The script is then tedious and contrived.

Example

A client came to me for a consultation on a script that was getting tepid responses. In his story his character, Bob, wants to impress a beautiful woman and so he buys expensive tickets to a Lakers game. As an obstacle, he had Bob lose the tickets and look frantically for them at the office, at home, and in the car. My client thought that Bob's problem was escalating because Bob was getting more desperate with each place he looked, when really the story was getting less involving because it was repetitive. It was the same obstacle—lost tickets—over and over.

Instead of having Bob buy expensive tickets and then lose them, we looked for a way to show how desperate he was to impress this woman by doing something he normally wouldn't do.

I asked my client if he had ever done anything that he knew was wrong but went ahead and did it anyway. One of the things that he came up with from his own life was taking money from a roommate. We gave that to the character. Without asking, Bob "borrows" money from his roommate's wallet. Now we can see Bob's desperation—he does something he normally wouldn't do—and more important, there will be consequences.

Bob's roommate discovers the theft and throws out the tickets to get back at him. The consequence of that is Bob going through the garbage to find those tickets, and the consequences of that are that he arrives late to pick up his date, and he's filthy and stinking. Bob still has the problem of lost tickets, but his problem has successfully escalated, not merely repeated.

By following the consequences of your character's own actions and the reactions of the important characters around him, you will up the stakes in a meaningful way. You will have a story of consequence, and I mean that literally.

But you don't have to take my word for it. Watch any episode of *The Honeymooners* and you will see a masterful example of plot building entirely based on the consequences of the Central Character's actions. Nothing is forced or manipulated. Every plot turn comes about because of Ralph's actions in pursuit of a simple, tangible goal. That's one of the main factors making the show a perennial favorite and a true television classic. Jackie Gleason was a great star, but lots of shows with major stars in them fail. It's the star *in the story* that makes a show work.

9. TREATMENT

The treatment is the heavy lifting of writing a television script. In the writing room we call it breaking the story. If you don't find your story in this phase, it will be harder, and probably impossible, to find later.

If we go back to the script-as-house metaphor, a treatment is the frame of the house and if the framework isn't sturdy, no matter what beautiful color you paint it, the house will collapse. Don't be in a hurry to move on from your treatment. Get your story laid out in the treatment and you will have a lot more fun writing your draft. I've rewritten treatments for TV episodes a dozen times before going to script.

Okay, so it's important.

What Is It?

A treatment is your story in simple narrative prose that tells what happens from beginning to end. No scenes. No dialogue.

No long descriptions. Just your story. Keep it short. About two pages for a half-hour episode; about four for a one-hour. <u>Double spaced</u>.

The fastest I ever had to turn around a script was on *The Mommies*. A script had to be completely scrapped and an entirely new story had to be conceived, developed, and written in five days. The task was assigned to me and my then partner, Cindy Chupack. We were exempt from all other duties that week, and we never left our office, not even for lunch—not a sacrifice I make easily.

I don't remember what the episode was about, but what I do remember is that we spent three days on story development—writing the treatment and outline—and two days writing the dialogue. The point is that we didn't rush the development stage—well, we rushed, we had to—but we didn't skip any of the steps.

The story treatment was more important than ever. I believe that if you must cut corners, the later in the process you do so, the better off you are.

As with the synopsis, don't cheat the length. Keeping your treatment within the range prescribed is part of what makes it such a useful tool. If you put in too much stuff you defeat the purpose, which is to see how your story works.

Start your treatment by writing your Premise Line. If it wasn't brief before, make it brief now. It's going to be your point of reference as you write your story out, and you don't need to wade through a lot of fuzzy details every time you want to remind yourself what you're writing about. If, as you write, you discover your story evolving in new ways, you may need to adjust your Premise Line to reflect the changes. That's fine; that's the development process in action.

I found this Premise Line for "No Fat" in my early development notes.

```
Ray is upset when the traditional family
Thanksgiving at the Barones is threatened
because Marie is cooking heart-healthy food
to lower cholesterol.
```

As you can see, I hadn't figured everything out yet. So don't worry if your Premise Line isn't all there yet either. Just start with whatever you know so far. As I developed my story and discovered how it was going to play out, I continued to adjust the line. In a later draft of the treatment my Premise Line reads:

```
The Barone family Thanksgiving is threatened
when Marie cooks a heart-healthy dinner and
Ray insults her by ordering a traditional
meal from a restaurant.
```

ABC

The primary purpose of your treatment is to lay out the overall narrative of your "A" story. An "A" story is the main story line that follows your Central Character. Some half-hour shows have only an "A" story. "B" stories are smaller, secondary stories. They usually involve supporting characters' problems that can be related to the "A" story or completely separate. One-hour dramas will usually have "B" and even "C" story lines that feature the supporting characters running along with the "A" story. The more of an ensemble your show is, the more important the "B" and "C" stories are.

Your treatment can include elements of your "B" story, but beware: it's easy to get distracted by "B" stories. Your focus should be on getting your "A" story working, then weave your "B" story around it.

No Dialogue

Dialogue is not action. What characters do is action. What happens because of what they do is story. Dialogue rides on action, but it is not in and of itself action. Action, not dialogue, is what you want in your treatment.

To illustrate this, let me cite the 2005 Writers Guild Award for best television comedy: *Curb Your Enthusiasm*. Now, what's interesting is that *Curb Your Enthusiasm* is famous for not having scripts! And yet the community of professional screenplay and television writers have chosen it as the best-written show on television.

What has been recognized here is that television writing is in the story structure, not in the dialogue. *Curb Your Enthusiasm* has no standard pages with dialogue, but what it does have is a highly developed and very specific outline that the actors and director follow. The characters are all played by expert improv actors who can create spontaneous dialogue when they have a strong structure to follow, and the result is a pretty brilliant story that has very few jokes but is often hilariously funny because the story works. Even if you don't like Larry David or the humor's not to your taste, the story structure is undeniable and worth studying.

Beat Sheet

As a preliminary step to writing your treatment, you can do something called a beat sheet. It is a bullet-point list of important plot incidents rather than a narrative. I think a particularly useful way to do a beat sheet is to start each beat with your Central Character's name.

TOOL BOX

> Tell your story in a list of main actions and begin each beat in your list with your Central Character's name.

It may seem awkward at first, but it will help you keep your Central Character driving the story. When you run into a beat that seems to be about another character, even if it's part of your "A" story, examine it and figure out how that event affects your Central Character; then rephrase the beat in terms of your Central Character's reaction.

Using "No Fat" again as an example, if I write a beat like this:

```
Debra shows Marie a magazine with a tofu
turkey recipe.

Marie takes the recipe for tofu turkey.
```

Ray is not implied in the action. So he's not driving. When I go to work this beat into a scene, I might do this scene without Ray at all. Isn't that okay? Maybe, but if this were my spec script, I'd check my research charts and I'd see that Ray is in almost every scene. I'll have a stronger script if he's in this scene.

So I'll take this same beat and rephrase it in terms of how it affects Ray, like this instead:

```
Ray discovers Debra giving Marie a recipe
for tofu turkey.
```

Now I'm focused on Ray's story line and it could lead me to his next actions, like this:

```
Ray pleads with Marie to make the tradi-
tional feast he's used to even if it means
blowing her diet. Ray shushes Debra when she
tries to support Marie. Ray is so unhappy
about Marie's healthy Thanksgiving plans, he
orders a traditional meal from a restaurant.
```

Ray does something that will turn the story. Ray is driving a story that could easily have slipped into a story that Marie was driving.

Couldn't I have gotten to this without phrasing the beats in terms of Ray? Possibly, but that's like saying, Couldn't I have pounded that nail in the wall without a hammer? Well, yes, I guess you could use your shoe or something else hammerlike, but if you've got a hammer, why not use it?

Exercise—Go on Location

So far we've been looking to our own personal experiences for inspiration and ideas. Now I'm going to suggest that you get out of your own world and explore the physical world your characters live in. Whatever you're writing about, go there.

If you're writing a *Grey's Anatomy*, go to a hospital and sit in the ER waiting area. Observe what's happening. How are the injured being brought in, what do family members do while they wait? What conversations can you hear? How do the doctors behave?

If you're writing a *Two and a Half Men* story about picking up a girl in a singles bar, go to one. I know you've been to some (many) already, but you haven't been to one with the express purpose of observing. Writing a *My Name Is Earl* and you've never been to a trailer park? Go visit one. Take a walk around, introduce yourself to someone you meet there. Write down what you see and hear. What are the smells and how do things feel? Notice what you touch and what you avoid. Write it down—especially the ordinary things; they'll be the most useful. What do you hear people talking about? How do they express themselves? Write down dialogue that you hear.

There's no way to know how anything will get used in your script, but the tangible experience of being there will give dimension to your script in both conscious and instinctual choices. You'll pick up ideas that you could never have thought up at your desk. You'll discover telling details that you can give to your characters that add authenticity and texture to your story.

As you write your treatment, you will need to keep story structure in mind. In the next chapter, I will give you a simple format to guide you in shaping your story.

10. STORY STRUCTURE

I have a chart that I give clients who come to me for story consultations. It is my adaptation of a chart that Mark Ganzel, a truly gifted writer I worked with on *Coach,* made up.

Mark was funny, generous, and a great inspiration, and he died much too young. He used to quote Woody Allen, who said "Eighty percent of success is showing up," and then confess, "I've never missed a single day of work. I'm afraid to! I know if I don't show up, the work will go on without me and I don't want anyone to discover that." He laughed when he said it, but he wasn't kidding.

One day Mark came in to work and presented everybody with a one-page chart that he felt summed up sitcom writing. When I saw it I felt like I had been given the key to a secret elixir. I thought the unpretentious way he got to the heart of what makes a story work was just brilliant. I lost my copy of Mark's chart years ago, but when I started script consulting I made up my own version based on what I remember of his. Here it is.

ELLEN SANDLER'S
SIMPLE, BUT NOT EASY, GUIDE TO CREATING
STORY STRUCTURE

Based on an Original Concept by Mark Ganzel

1. "Oh."
   "Mah Nish Tah Nah"
2. "The Little Uh Oh!"
3. "Ouch!"
4. "The Big Uh Ohhh!"
5. "Oh No!"
   "The Twist-a-Roo"
6. "Ah."

You can use this chart both at the beginning of your development to guide you in creating your story structure and later to assess the story you've come up with. If you're working on a story for a one-hour, add "Uh Ohs!" between the first "Uh Oh!" and "Ouch!" These additional "Uh Ohs!" are likely to turn out to be the Act Break moments for your script.

If you're doing an ensemble show and you have a "B" and even a "C" story line that runs parallel to the "A" story line, you can use this chart to structure those stories as well, keeping in mind that "B" and "C" stories will be less involved, with perhaps only one "Uh Oh!" and a small "Oh No!"

Okay, let's track the Story Structure Chart and see how useful it is:

"Oh."

Something happens that sets your story in motion. In academic terms that's called an Inciting Incident. I like "Oh." because I think of it as the moment when your audience goes, "Oh. That's interesting."

It's the event that catches your audience's attention and makes them want to stick around to see what happens. It's crucial to your story structure, but that doesn't mean your character has to know it's crucial, at least not just yet.

"Oh." can be as small as a broken zipper or as big as a corpse. If it's a corpse, you're probably writing a drama. But not necessarily—two of the funniest episodes in all of television start with a death. "The Kipper and the Corpse" episode of *Fawlty Towers* and the "Chuckles Bites the Dust" episode of *The Mary Tyler Moore Show*.*

"Mah Nish Tah Nah"

We have already discussed how "why today?" strengthens "Oh." in your story. It's not a separate story beat, but an important structural element nevertheless.

---

*If you've never seen these episodes, please rent them or go to the Museum of Television to look at them. Television is such an immediate, what-have-you-done-lately medium, it's easy to forget anything that came before yesterday. I encourage you to make the effort to be aware of TV's cultural history. It's important to realize that it is possible for television to be brilliant and that sometimes it actually is. You'll be a better writer for acknowledging the best and knowing what you can aspire to.

"The Little Uh Oh!"

"The Little Uh Oh!" is not just the next thing that happens, it's something that your Central Character wasn't expecting, and it changes things. Most story analysts call it a Turning Point because that's what it does, it turns the story in a new direction. I like "Uh Oh!" because it hits you in the gut and implies emotion. In "No Fat," "Uh Oh!" happens when Ray finds out Marie is not cooking turkey for Thanksgiving.

If you're having trouble finding a strong Turning Point, look at your opposing character's actions. The following exercise will help you explore.

Exercise—10 Alternatives

Focus on the supporting character for this exercise. Choose a turning point in your story and make a list of 10 alternative actions for the supporting character. See how the changed behavior will affect your Central Character's response.

There's a temptation to do a list like this in your head, but if you do you are more likely to quit early. If you write it down you'll have the visual data to keep you generating to the goal of ten. It might be faster if you do it in your head, but you'll forget a lot. You won't have the benefit of looking over your list later and considering some surprising combinations.

Don't overthink it. You want to do this quickly, to engage your creative, free-associating brain, and like in the cluster exercise, the less you think and manipulate, the better it will go. So set a timer for two or three minutes and don't judge any possibility while you do the exercise. A bad idea can lead to a good one. You won't know what's good or bad till you get there.

The first way might turn out to be the best, but how would you know if you don't try out some other possibilities? Think of it like shopping. You don't buy the first pair of shoes you see; you look around the whole store, see what's available, and reject most of them.* Do the same with your ideas.

Here's an example from a spec *Desperate Housewives* script that a writer consulted me on. The "Little Uh Oh!" comes after Susan breaks the news to her daughter that she wants to sell their house. It's a Turning Point for Susan because her daughter's resistance makes her change her plans.

The first response my client had was for the daughter to object verbally, to argue with Susan. Okay, it gets the information across that the daughter's unhappy, but is it enough of an obstacle to make Susan change her plans and is it interesting enough to keep an audience's attention?

I asked my client how she herself responds to bad news. She said, "I run away." Well, that was already a more interesting way for the daughter to react.

Then I asked her to write down ten ways the daughter might run away. At first she could think of only one way, literally getting up and running out of the room. Then I said okay, running away is escaping. What are other ways to escape? She came up with: 1. Ignore the news by silently continuing to eat, 2. Ask her mother to pass the salt, 3. Pick up a magazine to read, 4. Call the waiter, 5. Excuse herself politely and go to the ladies' room.

This is where she stalled. She was sure there were no more. I said keep going and make them less likely, even dumb. You don't have to be logical or on-story for the exercise. So she continued with 6. Sing, 7. Have a tantrum, 8. Cry, 9. Throw up, 10. Faint.

Surprised? She was. Any one of these responses would give the writer a more forceful consequence for Susan to deal with,

---

*Okay, if you're a guy, substitute camera equipment for shoes.

and create a more believable reason for the audience to understand why Susan would consider changing her plan. Out of this list the writer picked number 9, throw up. I thought it was great!

When she wrote the scene, she even used a couple of other items on her list for texture. The scene starts with the daughter singing (number 6), which gives her a bigger mood change at the end, and she gulps down tears (number 8) just before she throws up. Instead of three pages of realistic dialogue, what she ended up with was a scene that ran less than half a page and had a powerful visual metaphor so we, the audience, got the message fast and big—Susan's got a problem, her move is not going to go well.

"Ouch!"

This is the moment of greatest jeopardy for the Central Character and it is usually where you put your Act Break. How does your Central Character get into the most serious trouble? It doesn't have to be an explosion or a fight. It could be the tiny click of a door lock as your character stands naked in the hall, or the discovery of a tiny sock that confirms a missing child, or Marie's face when she discovers Ray ordered restaurant food. Serious trouble. It's a painful moment for your Central Character.

Executives will frequently critique a story by saying "the stakes aren't high enough," and when they do, this is the area that needs attention. How can you intensify the potential and make it more serious for your character? How can you make it more painful, more fearful for him?

Here's how I got to "Ouch!" in "No Fat." Early in my development process, I thought I would show Ray ordering from a restaurant. I tried a few ways: I could show Ray on the phone ordering—no, phone's boring. I could show him at a restaurant placing an order—no, that would mean an extra set just to place an order, not worth it. Ray could take the family out to eat for Thanksgiving (again, an extra set, but at least this amount of action would justify it), or he could eat the restaurant food at home before they go to Marie's for her tofu dinner.

But no, that avoids the real issue. The restaurant dinner has to be in Marie's face and Ray has to be there to catch the flack that results—bingo, the food has to get delivered to Marie's house just as they're sitting down to eat the tofu turkey. And here we are at . . . "Ouch!"

Since these are techniques, not formulas, every story will develop differently. The way it works in one is not necessarily how it will work in another. You have to be able to face the void and not know for a while. Explore and go with something. See if it leads you to the next story structure element. . . .

"The Big Uh Ohhh!"

This is the thing that is even more frightening than "Ouch!" In "No Fat," as uncomfortable as Ray is facing his mom after he insulted her by ordering restaurant food, he is even more afraid of Debra's disapproval (the threat of no sex always hangs over Ray). Plus she takes the food away and he's not going to get it anyway. "The Big Uh Ohhh!" is what pushes your Central Character to go on and face his fear in . . .

"Oh No!"

This is what the whole story is about. The technical term is the Climax or Confrontation scene. It's a confrontation between your Central Character and whichever of the supporting characters has been his biggest opposition in the story. It's when they come face-to-face—and I do mean face-to-face; don't do it on the phone or in a letter, or, weakest of all, overheard by accident.

This is where the reason everything that's been happening comes to a head. This is where your Central Character resolves the story. And to reiterate, it must be your Lead who resolves it. If you let another character take care of things or solve the problem for him, you take all the power out of your story. It's like letting the air out of a large balloon. Not a pretty sound, and not the sound you want readers to hear when they get to the end of your script.

Your Central Character doesn't have to win for it to be a successful resolution dramatically. She can lose her case but achieve a moral victory. She can just flat-out lose, as long as she went to battle and fought to the end.

In the confrontation in "You Bet," Ray exposes Frank for using him to win bets. Frank never apologizes, or even admits he was wrong, but Ray did the courageous thing by standing up to him and that was enough for a satisfying ending.

"The Twist-a-Roo"

This is the note of irony that makes the story funny or poignant, something that gives us an insight into human nature. In the same way that *Mah Nish Tah Nah* is closely related to "Oh.", the

"Twist-a-Roo" is closely related to "Ah." In "No Fat" the "Twist-a-Roo" comes when Marie gets caught eating the turkey leg in Ray's kitchen in the middle of the night. And if you want to see why Doris Roberts has won five Emmys, watch this scene on video. It's a perfect example of how an actor can turn something into much more than the writer imagined. The actors don't make it up as they go along, but a terrific actor can add magic to what's written on the page.

"Ah."

In a series you want your characters back to so-called normal at the end of the episode. The academic term is the Resolution. I call it "Ah." because the audience can feel a sigh of relief, "Ahhh, we're home, nothing's changed, it's safe to tune in next time." Often in a comedy show, you do it with a funny twist on what just happened. In "No Fat" everybody winds up at the table eating turkey together.

Your first draft of your treatment is probably going to be sketchy and full of story holes. That's okay, because you get to rewrite as many times as you want. Actually, *more* than you want. A lot more.

11. REWRITING YOUR TREATMENT

> NO QUITTING halfway through because "it's not working." You get nothing from an unfinished project, and you learn nothing.
> —STEPHEN J. CANNELL, *ROCKFORD FILES*,
> *THE A TEAM, HUNTER, WISEGUY*

This is the hard part. You're not going to want to go back in there. It means pulling things apart that you struggled to put together, and that's going to be painful. But still you must. It's doubtful that your story works the first time through. I've never done it, and no client I've ever worked with has.

Okay, let's say you're willing, but where do you start? You've done the best you could; if you knew how to do it differently, you would have. Here's a Rewrite Kit full of tools that I've used to bring fresh air to my own work and that of my clients and students. You don't have to use them all, but I think you'll find at least a few that will open some windows and let the sun shine in.

A New Perspective

Can you identify where the weaknesses are? One place to look is the middle of your story. That's usually where the biggest problem is. Is it flat, repetitive, and not escalating? Stephen Cannell is one of the best storytellers in the business and he has said, "Plot from the heavy's point of view in Act Two." I love this advice, and I use it all the time. I don't know if I do it as well as he does, but it never fails to improve a story. Here's how it works for me:

Up to now we have focused on the Central Character and his driving force. Now shift your perspective and find out what's on the opposing character's agenda. You will not need to develop as much story for her as you have for your Central Character, but if you define her goals and track what she is doing to pursue them, you will also create meaningful complications for your Central Character.

Example

I was consulting with a writer who was struggling with a story line for his pilot. His Central Character was a teacher at a private school who wanted to change the grading process. He came up against the headmaster, who refused to implement the change. The writer then had the teacher redouble his efforts by going around the headmaster and uniting the other teachers to back his plan. It worked, and the grading process was forced on the headmaster.

This seems like an escalation, but it didn't have any meaningful consequence for the Central Character. The character was still in the same place; nothing had gotten worse for him. No turning point. He started out wanting something, went for it, and got it. He didn't have to change or grow in any way.

I suggested to the writer that we consider what the headmaster's actions might be. What if, instead of the teacher being successful in getting his plan through, the headmaster fires the teacher for undermining his authority? This proud, arrogant teacher now has to do something very difficult for him—he has to apologize, admit error, and fight to keep the job he thought he was too good for. The turning point is what makes this into a story.

By creating an agenda for the opposing character, you create more interesting action for the Central Character and reveal more of his character.

Leading Questions

How are my supporting characters integrated into the story?

What is the relationship of the other characters to your Central Character's goal? Supportive or opposing? Who's trouble? Who's an ally? Please don't make the supporting characters "tools." Even though they're secondary, they must be people with some purpose of their own.

Remember Newman on *Seinfeld*? He was a minor character, but every time he appeared he had an agenda of his own. The writers didn't use him to conveniently provide an obstacle for Jerry. Newman always had his own reasons, which then consequently resulted in a problem for Jerry.

On police detective shows, there's a lot of exposition and factual details to reveal; therefore, characters are used as sounding boards to get that information out. However, if you give that supporting character even a small agenda of his own, the scene will play stronger and the expositional information won't feel so clunky. Let's say you've got an explanation of DNA results to get across to the audience. So you have your lead detective give the information to the lawyer. Well, it will be more dynamic if the lawyer is late for court and the detective has to work to keep his attention.

How does my Lead resolve the story?

What is the event—it should be near the end—when what your story is about is specifically dealt with? Who's involved? It should be your Central Character and her chief opponent. Have you got another character stepping in and solving the problem or the case? If your Lead is not resolving your story, you must restructure your story so that she does.

How has my Central Character changed by the end of the story?

In a television episode it will be a small lesson that won't affect the basic nature of the character, as opposed to a movie, where it will probably be life-changing. But there must be some change or there will be no point to your story, which will leave your audience (reader) wondering, "Why did we go through all that?" If you've got your Central Character successfully resolving your story, then you probably have created a sufficient change as well.

Surprise!

Not a big surprise ending. The surprises I suggest you look for are the little ones that happen throughout the story. Do the characters do something they don't usually do? For example, comfort someone they usually avoid, or ask advice of someone they usually don't trust? In "No Fat," Debra supports Marie against Ray; that was unusual for her but believable in the context of that story.

Surprising behavior must be strongly set up and clearly motivated, because surprises in a script play best if they are also inevitable. It's easy to create a surprise if you grab something

unrelated or illogical. It's a fine technique to open up your head
and get you thinking in a fresh direction, as in the 10
Alternatives Exercise, but it's unlikely to work as an effective
tactic in your story structure. It will be surprising, but it will
also most likely be confusing.

Red Flags

I love red flags, because they make rewriting so easy. Wait, no,
rewriting isn't easy. But red flags make finding out *where* you
need to rewrite easy. I'll show you how to see them and it will
be like finding Waldo after you know where he is. You won't be
able to *not* see him.

Don't tell when you can . . .

This is my favorite red flag: TELL. The simple word "tell."
When you're looking over your story treatment and you see
where you've written Character A tells Character B . . . anything. What you're really doing is writing dialogue without actually writing it, and that doesn't help you move your story. As I
said before, in a treatment or any developmental step prior to
the actual script, you want to avoid dialogue.

I know, dialogue is fun. It's why most writers want to write
in the first place. Dialogue will be the wings on which your
story will fly eventually, but when you're working out your
structure, dialogue slows you down. If you describe a beat of
your story as one character telling something to another, you
have shortchanged yourself on emotional content. Plus, when
you do go to write the dialogue later, it is likely to come out predictable or what is called "on the nose."

It's okay if you used "tell" or even an actual line of dialogue the first time through, but consider it a placeholder. On this next pass, investigate. Find out what's behind that dialogue. What is the motivator? Instead of the character merely telling, go deeper, get under that message and include what the character is doing by telling.

For example, let's take a hypothetical scene for *Desperate Housewives*. If you've written in your treatment "Edie tells Susan her house is messy," when you go to write your script you're likely to write something like this:

```
          EDIE
     Susan, your house is such a mess, I
     could give you the number of my or-
     ganizer.


          SUSAN
     Oh, that's really nice of you, but
     this way I know where everything is.
```

It's okay. It sounds like real people talking and it certainly gets the information across. Edie is definitely telling Susan her house is messy, but it feels generic—not bad, but not special either. Certainly not enough to separate your spec script from all the others the agent's assistant has to read this week.

What if you change "tell" to "criticize"? Now your treatment reads, "Edie criticizes Susan's housekeeping." Immediately your beat is more alive. There's intention, emotional action, and reaction implied. It's jumping off the page. When it comes time for you to write the actual dialogue for the scene, you'll have so much more to work with. Now when you go to write your draft you'll be more likely to write something like this.

```
          EDIE
     Well, I'd like to sit down, but all
     the chairs seem to be in use.
```

                    SUSAN
Oh, just throw that stuff on the
floor.

                    EDIE
(tiny pause)
Interesting.

                    SUSAN
Look, Edie, if you came over here
to criticize my housekeeping—

                    · EDIE
(feigning innocence)
What? I didn't say anything.

                    SUSAN
Oh yes you did. You said "interesting."

                    EDIE
Interesting is not a criticism.

                    SUSAN
It is when you take that little
pause and pretend like you're not
going to say anything.

The action and emotional intention in the verb opens up
much fresher content for your scene. Knowing that Edie wants
to "criticize" automatically makes me create a context—I have to
imagine something for her to criticize. Suddenly I see stuff lying
around on the chairs. If I'm thinking Edie has to tell Susan
something, my imagination isn't engaged. I'm just focused on
what she has to say.

Giving Edie the intention to criticize does something else for you. It builds in a frisson of emotional conflict. She wants to criticize, but she knows that's not nice and so attempts to re-strain herself, and says, "Interesting." The inherent conflict is what makes the moment feel fresh and alive.

Here we have Edie with specific dialogue that doesn't sound anything like any other episode, yet it is completely in character. A whole script written with this kind of emotional content feels fresh and is fun to read. All this by changing "tells" to "criticizes."

No, I didn't know all this when I sat down and wrote that run of dialogue. I just wrote from the action "criticize." The analysis came afterward. You don't need to analyze the beat; us-ing emotionally active verbs does all that for you.

TOOL BOX

> Go through your story treatment and highlight every in-stance where you have characters telling, asking, or ex-plaining something to each other. You'll become aware of how often you rely on what is essentially dialogue to tell your story. Now replace those verbs with emotion-ally active verbs and watch your story come alive.

You tell the story; your characters do anything but. I keep a list of active verbs. Whenever I come across an emotionally charged verb that describes a way that someone communicates, I make a note. That way I have lots of options to choose from when I need to replace "tell."*

Here're some from my list to get you started. . . .

---

*Watch out for other words, like "asks," "says," or "explains," that are dia-logue indicators in the same way "tells" is and will serve you better if re-placed with emotionally active verbs.

Don't have your character **Tell** when they can...

Betray

Attack

Tattle

Confess

Belittle

Divulge

ADMIT

Confide

LIE TO

Tell off

Hint at

𝕿𝖎𝖙𝖎𝖑𝖑𝖆𝖙𝖊

Harangue

Tip off

Tease

Mislead

Argue with

Accuse

Cajole

Bemoan

CRITICIZE

Blame

Denounce

Beg

Demand

Decisions

I see this all the time; a writer will describe a character's action as "Meredith decides to go see her mother." Cut the decision—that takes place in the character's head—go right to the action. Go to what your character does *after* she's decided: "Meredith drives like a maniac to the nursing home."

Here's another example: "Robin decides it's time she stood up for herself and asks Ted to do the dishes." (Double red flags: "decides" and "asks" in one sentence.) Here's a more active version: "Robin slams out of the house, leaving Ted with a sink full of dishes." Deciding is mental, it's hard to photograph. Action is visual, and that's what needs to be on your page.

Trying too hard

Characters are always "trying" to do something. I see it in everybody's work, mine included. You're going to write it, that's okay. Notice when you do, and then get rid of it. Whenever you've got your character "trying" to do something, think of those Nike ads and have them just do it! They can have a hard time, they can struggle, they can fail, and then they can try, oops, I mean, *do* something else. "Allison tries to convince Joe to dress up for the party." Weak. Go straight to the action: "Allison begs Joe to change clothes." Or even more active: "Allison surprises Joe with a gift of a new shirt and jacket and then hints at sex after the party." If you see a line like this in your treatment, I guarantee the scene you write will be more exciting, active, and alive than the one you'd write based on "tries to convince."

You may be thinking, "Can't I make up that kind of action when I'm actually writing the scene?" Yes, you can, but the question is, will you? Once you start writing dialogue, you want it to flow. Having worked out the emotional action will allow you to do that. Your dialogue will sparkle with spontaneity, and not only that, the emotional action you've set up will spark even more actions when you are actually writing the scene.

The meaning of "is" is

Turn whatever your character "is" thinking/feeling/doing into emotions and actions. If you've written, "Lynette is pissed off because Tom is watching TV," go for the action: "Lynette attacks Tom for watching TV while she's working her ass off."

Nothing more than feelings

I've said it before, I'll say it again: Feeling is not action. Your job as a writer is to translate your character's feelings into action.

What does your character do when he feels something? If you write "George is angry because Callie dumped him," write this instead: "George rips up Callie's note and throws the pieces at himself in the mirror." We'll know he's angry and hurt.

If you've written "Brenda is frustrated when she can't get in the door," it's okay, but you'll find more action if you push past it into how that feeling makes her behave: "Brenda kicks the locked door and breaks her foot." Then, you might discover more action when "Brenda lies about how she broke her foot."

Thinks

Change "Keith thinks Veronica is up to something" to "Keith sneaks into Veronica's room and rifles through her desk." Or, since Veronica is your Central Character, write it from her point of view: "Veronica catches Keith going through her desk."

You're not going to use all of these tools all of the time. They won't all work in every situation, but they will help you develop plot and story through character and lead you to a more exciting way to create a story.

Go Back to the Beginning

After each rewrite of your treatment, revisit your Premise Line and ask yourself again, "What is my story about?" Rework your Premise Line to incorporate your new version of your story.

So, is your narrative story in good shape? Do you like it? Do you still want to do it? I hope so, because you've done the heavy lifting; you've "broken the story." Congratulations. Uh, wait, don't pull up your Final Draft window. No dialogue yet. Got to make an outline first.

12. THE OUTLINE

What's the difference between a treatment and an outline? The outline has scene breakdowns and it will be longer than a treatment. In the treatment you were laying out significant story beats about what happens. In the outline, you get more specific about *how* the story happens. You are really constructing your script at this point. Keeping to our analogy of a house, if the treatment is the framework, think of the outline as the walls and floors.

Outline Format

Basic format for an outline is a slug line* identifying each scene, followed by a paragraph describing the important action of the

---

*Slug lines indicate a new scene and identify the scene's location and time. They are always in all caps and, depending on your format, underlined or not. Multi-camera, underlined; single camera, not. They look like this: INT. KITCHEN - DAY.

scene in narrative prose. Use short sentences. Make them punchy, readable, and amusing, but not cute. No quirky fonts. Use only 12 point Courier New or Courier Final Draft and begin numbering outline pages on page 2.

TOOL BOX

SCENE NUMBERING SITCOM STYLE

Scenes in a multi-camera sitcom are usually identified by letters. The few exceptions are shows that are shot on videotape. Those scenes are numbered, 1, 2, 3, and so on. But most multi-camera shows are shot on film stock with four film cameras mounted on pedestals that move around the sound stage. For these shows, the scenes are designated with a special sequence of letters that you need to know about. The scenes go A, B, C, D, E—so far so good, but now there's no Scene F and no Scene G. You pick up with H, then no I, J is okay as are K, L, and M, no N, no O, P's okay, and by this point you probably aren't writing any more scenes in a half-hour script.

These letters are skipped because of similarities to other letters or numbers. The cameras in a multi-camera show move to marks on the floor for their shooting positions during the filming of a scene. These marks are identified by the scene letter followed by a number for the order of positions within that scene. The guys who move the cameras have to look at the floor, see the marks, and move the cameras to them. When you're following a character, those moves can come pretty fast. There's a real possibility that an F could be mistaken for an E or an O for a C, which would land the camera in the wrong spot. Seems weird until you know the reason; then it makes good sense.

When laying out your scenes in the outline, if you are working in multi-camera format, you will have a teaser followed by scenes designated by letter. In single-camera format you will have only slug lines, no scene numbers or letters.

Focus Lines

Just as you developed a Premise Line for your story, I suggest you do the same thing for each scene. For scenes I call them Focus Lines so as to distinguish them from your overall story Premise Line. The Focus Line identifies the key thing that must happen in the scene.

Write your Scene Focus Line right under your slug line and then follow that with a brief narrative description of what happens in the scene. A Focus Line does not have to be expressed as action. For example, in "No Fat," my Focus Line for the teaser is: "Establish Thanksgiving." In single-camera format you may have some very short scenes for which the Focus Line may be all you need.

WARNING: Use Focus Lines for your work purposes only. If you are writing on assignment, you will be expected to turn in an outline for notes and approval. DO NOT INCLUDE YOUR FOCUS LINES IN THE VERSION YOU SUBMIT TO THE SHOWRUNNER OR STUDIO EXECUTIVES. They won't know what it is and it will confuse them.

A likely source for Scene Focus Lines is your beat sheet—with adjustments, of course, as some story beats will have changed by this stage. As in your beat sheet, your Focus Lines should be from your Central Character's point of view. If you discover that the key event of the scene is not clearly affecting your main character, you may want to question why that scene is there and then either cut it or reshape it.

However, if you have a plot with several story lines, some that follow other characters, it may be a justification for scenes that exclude your Central Character. If you are writing an ensemble piece like *Desperate Housewives*, follow the same process for each separate story line, keeping that character in the driver's seat of their story line.

Now that you know what your scene is intended to accomplish, how do you create the action to do it?

The Teaser

You can use the Story Structure Chart as a guide for what has to happen in your scenes. For example, "Oh." = what happens in the first scene. In a single-camera show, like *Scrubs* or *The Closer,* "Oh." may spread out over a short sequence of scenes.

Since you are writing a spec of an existing series, you don't have to introduce the characters or the basic premise of the show, but you do have to set up the problem that will be the driving force of this story in the opening scene or scenes. This is known as the teaser, because it is shown before the first commercial to entice the audience into watching the show.

One-hour dramas use their teasers to set up the problem. For example, in a police procedural, we'll find out immediately what the crime is or who's missing.

With sitcoms the teaser (also called a cold open, depending on the show) can either be the beginning of your main story or a short, funny, stand-alone scene that doesn't have anything to do with the subsequent story. If that's the case with your show, then consider the "A" scene your first scene and that will be where you introduce the story setup.*

Since the *Mah Nish Tah Nah* factor is closely connected to, maybe even inseparable from "Oh.", that's going to be set up in either the teaser or the first scene too.

As you study your research, you will discover that the story setup is often fairly ritualized. It can be very specific, such as the special effect disappearance at the end of the teaser of *Without a Trace*, or it can be as loose as it simply happens at the end of the first scene. Whatever it is, you must do it exactly as the show does it. If the setup for the story happens on the same page in each episode you studied, make yours happen there too. This is where your diligent research pays off. Study the range and follow the stylistic rituals closely.

By all means consult your research numbers for other aspects you'll need to follow, like: How long does the "A" scene run? Who's always in it? Who's usually in it? You aren't looking to copy another episode, you're looking for the pattern of elements that are in all episodes to guide you as you structure your scene. Go to the experts—the scripts—for that help.

Where Are We?

If you've concentrated on story beats and resisted the temptation to lay out scenes in your treatment, you now have a chance to think creatively about where to set your action.

---

*At *Raymond* we had the option; some teasers related to the show, some didn't. Many times we would write a stand-alone teaser but later it would be cut. This was usually done for time. If the show ran long, we could pick up a minute or so by cutting the stand-alone teaser and using the beginning of the "A" scene as the teaser.

Don't settle for your first choice. Imagine the same action in different locales. You can always return to your first choice if a new place doesn't work as well. Ordinary action in a surprising locale can give your scene an extra dimension. It doesn't have to be an odd or wild location to be interesting. Take a scene about two people embarrassed to run into each other and move it from a coffee shop to, say, a church confessional. Ordinary action, ordinary location, but combining them makes it surprising and adds dramatic tension.

Yes, in a TV script you're limited to the regular sets of an established show, but you can still think about ways to use what you have creatively. What if Lynette is criticizing Tom for not helping with cleanup after a party? The kitchen seems like the obvious place. But what if she holds back and doesn't lash out at him until they're going to bed? The same story beat, and you're still using the regular sets, but it will be more interesting. It could certainly up the stakes if Tom is expecting to have sex and instead gets hit with his wife's anger. Be sure to let the new environment affect the scene; otherwise why bother to go there?

It can work the other way for you too. Since you need to conserve the number of swing sets* you use (check your research chart for what the usual number is on your show), if you've got too many outside locations, see how you can reset the action in a regular set.

In the first draft of "No Fat" there were two scenes set in Ray and Debra's bedroom, the teaser and a scene late at night when Ray and Debra hear a noise, which leads Ray to discover Marie in his kitchen eating the restaurant Thanksgiving dinner he ordered.

Even though Ray and Debra's bedroom was a regular set, it

---

*Term used for any new set. See Showbiz Meanings for Regular Words: A Selective Glossary.

wasn't a standing set* and we didn't have room on the stage for it that week. So we reset the teaser in the living room and ended up cutting the late-night scene altogether. The teaser played in the living room just fine, and instead of the late-night scene we picked up Ray already coming downstairs in the dark with a baseball bat and calling out to whoever is in the house.

The set practicalities led to a tighter script. We didn't need that scene in the bedroom to set up a prowler; we did it in one line and on an action—much better.

Scene Structure

Scenes are the building blocks with which you choose to tell your story. Like your story, scenes need narrative structure. Every scene needs to have, that's right, three interconnected elements:

1. Setup. (Beginning)

2. Power Switch. (Middle) This is the scene's turning point. Just like your story has turning points, your scenes will also have a turning point, or what I call a power switch.

3. Arrow. (End) The element that drives you to the next scene.

This is what will be in your narrative description of your scene. You could list these elements like a mini beat sheet if you

---

*A standing set is permanently set up and used in every show. Regular sets are already built and frequently used but are stored until needed. The economics of multi-camera shows depends on shooting everything in one night. The sets must be up and prelit, so the cameras that are on moving pedestals can roll quickly from one scene to the next. There is no time on a shoot night to take a set down and put up another, and a sound stage can only hold so many sets; thus the limits of even regular sets.

want to, and then turn it into a narrative description with specifics of how these beats happen.

Setup

Following the same pattern as your overall story development, the top of the scene is your setup. Here again you can ask *Mah Nish Tah Nah*—why is this happening right now? If you pin that down, your scene will have more definition.

Power Switch

Part two, the power switch, is exactly that. If the scene starts with your character in control, something has to happen that shifts her off balance by the end. Conversely, if she comes into a scene upset, she ends with some satisfaction. This is the part of the scene where your Central Character wins or loses, and if she wins in this scene, she should probably lose in the next one.

For example, if your Central Character is a detective and at the top of your scene she's got a guilty perp, she starts the scene in control. Through questioning she learns the perp is innocent; she got the wrong guy. She's lost some power.

Arrow

Each scene should have a compelling reason to move on to the next one. We want to see how your Central Character recovers if he lost power, or we're waiting to see if he can keep it if he gained power. That's what keeps your audience hooked in, and that's essential in a TV show. Identify the scene's arrow for yourself. The more specific you are about what the arrow is, the more you will be able to point it when you write your dialogue.

B Stories

In your treatment you were primarily concerned with the "A" story for your Central Character. If your show uses "B" stories, the outline is the place to develop them. Some shows start the "B" story in the "B" scene,* some start the "B" story in the "A" scene. Refer to your script research to determine what your show does.

When you are including a "B" story point in a scene, begin the scene with it. The "A" story point is more important, and you want it to carry the scene. Putting "B" story elements after the "A" story will feel anticlimactic and stuck on. Instead of supporting your main story, it will hold it up.†

Exercise—Teeter-totter

Take your outline and reduce it to just the slug lines and Focus Lines. Then graph a simple teeter-totter. Put your Central

---

*When I first started writing TV I thought it was called the "B" scene because that's where you did the "B" story. Then I noticed that some shows started the "B" story in the "A" scene and other shows didn't have a "B" story at all. That's when I realized this was not a logical process.
†Supporting and holding up usually mean the same thing, but in story terms *supporting* and *holding up* are opposites. Language is funny, isn't it?

Character (CC) on one side and the Other character(s) (O) on the other side. What is the position at the top of the scene and what is it at the end of the scene?

If your Central Character starts out the scene frustrated or angry about something, your teeter-totter looks like this:

And if your Central Character gets some kind of satisfaction in the scene, at the end the teeter-totter looks like this:

Your Central Character gained power.

If your Central Character starts out fairly neutral, the teeter-totter looks like this:

at the beginning and if he then loses something or sustains a disappointment, the scene ends like this:

Your character has lost power, which is fine for your story.

However, you can look at this and think, I wonder how I can raise him at the beginning so he has farther to fall (more to lose) by the end of the scene.

If your teeter-totter looks like this:

at the beginning and still looks like this:

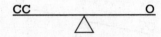

at the end, you know you'd better do something more with your scene and you have some idea where to start: ask yourself what you can do to intensify the situation so that your character starts the scene either lower or higher.

If you do this for your whole outline you will have an instant visual guide that will easily track the literal ups and downs of your character's journey toward his goal. If you see that your character starts a lot of scenes in neutral, take that as an indication that your character doesn't care enough—now ask yourself, "Why do I care about this issue?" Push yourself to dig deep. When you know why you care, you'll have something to give your character.

If you see that your Central Character ends a lot of scenes on an upswing, things may be going too easily for her. Why? Can you strengthen her obstacles? Or give her an emotional issue that would make things harder, i.e., more interesting, more involving for the audience? Can her fear be stronger? Not necessarily bigger, but more real for her (you)? You don't have to go rummaging deep in her psychic past for this. Keep it in the present.

Grey's Anatomy did an entire "B" story about Cristina's fear of apologizing to another doctor. It was unbearably hard for her, and we didn't have to go back to her childhood to find out why. It was compelling enough to see how her fear manifested itself in the present; we saw her resistance and her struggle, and we believed it. We didn't have to know all the backstory to believe it was hard for her.

If your character ends a lot of scenes down, then what's keeping him going after his goals? He needs a few successes for encouragement to keep the story going. Then you have the suspense factor of whether it's going to go wrong again, which in a drama can be terrifying, or in a comedy, funny.

The Time Is Now

The narrative in an outline is always—and this is a rule—*always* written in present tense. You are writing what will be seen and filmed (someday maybe!) as it happens.

I don't write:

```
After Frank opened the door a delivery guy
brought in a huge box of take-out food.
```

I write:

```
Frank opens the door to reveal a delivery
guy with a huge box of take-out food.
```

Nothing that happened in the past can be filmed now in this scene. If you're writing *Without a Trace* or *Medium* some scenes will be flashbacks, but after you indicate that it is a flashback scene in your slug line,* you will still describe the action in present tense. That's the point of the flashback, to see it happen.

Don't write what's going to happen in the future either, even if it's 30 seconds into the future. Write it as it happens.

———————

*It will look like this: INT — MOTEL ROOM — DAY — FLASHBACK

For example, don't write:

```
Joe gets a letter that will reveal the name
of the doctor he's been looking for.
```

Wait till you get there. In this scene you write:

```
Joe grabs his mail on the way out.
```

In the next scene you write:

```
Joe reads a letter that reveals the name of
the doctor who killed his wife.
```

How long should your outline be? It's a question of style. I think shorter is better, because I like to use the outline for overview. Some showrunners will want a very long, detailed outline before allowing you to go to script, but on a spec script it's your choice.

Many writers include lines of dialogue in their outlines. It's not wrong, but I suggest you stay away from dialogue in the outline for the same reasons as I've stated for the treatment. It goes double for jokes. If you put a joke in your outline you're going to want to write to that joke, and writing to a joke usually makes for contrived action and forced dialogue. Build the comedy through character development, growing frustrations, worsening situations. A joke that flows naturally from the developing scene will be funnier, I promise you.

There is one exception, and it's a big one. If your showrunner gives you a joke or a line of dialogue in notes, use it! Put it in your outline. Your job will be to make it feel organic later when you have to write it into the dialogue. It's hard, but it's what makes you a valuable asset to an Executive Producer.

In your own outline for a spec script, do yourself a favor: leave out the jokes and dialogue.

Feedback

When you have an outline you feel is working, it's time to show it to someone else and get some feedback. Adhere to the requirements of a professional-level document. Do not give anyone pages with handwritten notes, misspelled words, incorrect punctuation, or improper formatting. It's not respectful of your own work and it's not respectful of the reader's time.

Who should you show it to? You can show it to other writers whose work you like. You can show it to friends who are smart and care enough about you to give you an honest opinion. You can show it to a professional consultant for considered feedback and support.

> **God save me** from amateurs. They don't know what they are reading but it is much more serious than that. They immediately start rewriting. I never knew this to fail. It is invariable. . . . They have the authority of ignorance and that is something you simply cannot combat.
> —JOHN STEINBECK

When you give your work, at any stage of development, to someone else to read, what you want from them is simply response, not solutions. Ninety-nine percent of someone else's solutions to your story problems will be formulaic solutions anyway, and you don't need that.

You may want to get more than one person's opinion. If one person finds something off, well, that could be his problem. If three people cite a similar issue as confusing, you need to investigate and clarify the beat.

When you get feedback, listen. Just listen. Don't explain, and don't justify. If they don't understand something, explaining it to them will not help you improve your story outline, which is what this painful process is about. Showing your material to someone for feedback is not about approval (as nice as that is, and I hope there is a lot, as it will encourage you to continue). It is about finding out where your story is not working so you can fix it. So listen.

Rewrite

Now you have to rewrite. Look for the same red flags as you did in the treatment to help you focus your rewrite: tells, tries, decides, you know the drill. This is an opportunity to catch areas you didn't get to in the treatment and to go deeper with some you did touch on. Sure, it's a lot of work, but do you think it will get easier later when you're busy with dialogue and details? Do it now, and if you come up with something better in the course of writing the first draft, you can change it.

Check in with your research chart, and compare what you've got with what your chart indicates the show does. If you see an element that's not in your patterns, this is the time to fix it.

Prepare for a ripple effect. If you change something one place, it is likely that you're going to have to change some other things too. That's the point. Your story is all of a piece; the beats should be integrally connected. Maybe you've heard of what scientists call the "butterfly effect" to illustrate how things in nature are connected. So named because it refers to the idea that a butterfly flapping its wings in one part of the world can cause a tornado to occur in another part. I think of this as the writer's butterfly effect.

With this in mind, the point at which a story problem exists is usually not the point at which you fix it. Very often you cannot fix the problem in a later scene until you have addressed the setup in the first scene, but you wouldn't know that until you took the risk of putting it down on paper, where you could see it fail.

I encourage you to tackle major story problems in the outline stage, but I also want to caution you about the dangers of perfectionism. Yes, make your story work, but don't get hung up on it at this stage. It doesn't have to be perfect; it can't be—there is no "perfect" story.

If you've followed the form so far and you've got story beats that make sense to objective readers, you've got a good outline—keep going. It's important that you work through the whole process.

Sooo . . . Go to script!

13. THE SCRIPT

> Time now comes finally to move my book. . . . And
> I must forget even that I want it to be good. Such
> things belong only in the planning stage. Once it
> starts, it should not have any intention save only to
> be written.
>
> —JOHN STEINBECK

You are now ready to write DIALOGUE!! The reason you
probably wanted to write a spec script in the first place. You're
here. Your characters get to TALK! All that work you did in your
treatment and outline, where you made the effort to identify
motives, intentions, and actions instead of having your characters tell each other stuff—now they'll have lots to say. Let them.

Format

You are now going to write a rough draft, but even though it's
rough, you write it in correct format. It makes no sense to ever
write any draft of a TV script out of format.

If you are using a software writing program like Final Draft
or Movie Magic Screenwriter, it will offer you numerous choices
of TV show format styles. There's a good chance your show is
in the menu. But check your research. As I've said repeatedly,

your best guide to accurate formatting is a sample script from the show.*

The Exposition Truck

You will inevitably have to deal with exposition in your first scene. Exposition is information your audience needs to know in order to understand why things are happening. Most of your *Mah Nish Tah Nah* element will come out in exposition.

It's the backstory of your episode, so it's stuff that happened in the past, and that can get pretty clunky when you frontload it into the present tense. Signs of clunky exposition are:

- Using more than one name in a sentence. "Sharon told Paul to meet me at the pizza place."

- A phrase that starts with "Remember ..." or its variation, "Don't forget ..." "Remember, we have to go to Paul and Sharon's tonight."

- The phrase "I told you ..." As in, "I told you, I can't go with you tonight because I have to go to Sharon and Paul's anniversary party." Or, compounding the problem, "Remember, I told you I wasn't going to be able to go with you because ..."

- A long, run-on sentence with more information than any one person would care about. "I'm not making dinner

---

*Book page proportions are different from script page proportions; therefore, the sample dialogues used in this book approximate correct format but should not be used as exact guides. Better to consult one of the excellent formatting books listed in Appendix III: Sources.

tonight because we're meeting your brother Paul and his new girlfriend, Sharon, at the pizza place for their big one-month anniversary and we have to leave in five minutes or we'll be late and you know how Paul hates it when we don't respect his boundaries."

I've exaggerated, but not much. I see stuff like this all the time. And if you look carefully at your script, you'll probably spot some. I call this kind of dialogue a delivery from the Exposition Truck. I can almost hear it making those distinctive warning beeps as it backs up, getting ready to dump a load of exposition right in the middle of your scene. Listen to pretty much any TV show; you'll hear it from now on too.

It's not necessarily wrong. Writers do it because it's easy, especially when you are on a tight deadline, but for your spec script you really should do better. And you can.

Eight Ways to Stop the Exposition Truck

- **Cover the Information with a Joke.** The humor will take the edge off the obvious.

- **Give the Character Delivering the Information an Emotional Attitude.** You can say a lot of things in anger that would sound dull if you say them straight.

Here's an example from "No Fat" that uses a combination of these two techniques:

RAY

Why are you eating fake eggs?

MARIE

Because your father's cholesterol

is dangerously high. We had it

checked yesterday.

FRANK

It was lower than yours.

MARIE

One point lower!

FRANK

I'll still live longer than you.

MARIE

What? Thirty seconds?

FRANK

I'll take what I can get.

```
                    RAY

Hey, Romeo and Juliet, I just came

over to borrow a garbage bag.
```

- **Blend the Information in Later.** Maybe the audience doesn't need to know it all up front. Can you hold off on revealing it? It might be more effective and more active at a later point. You may discover you don't need it at all and then you can...

- **Leave It Out.** A lot of times you think the audience needs more background details than they actually do.

- **Make It Now.** Instead of having your character remind someone of something she already told him, make this time the first time she tells him. It will activate your moment. Another effective way to make "remember-when-I-told-you" dialogue present tense is to let your characters remember it differently and argue over *how* they remember whatever it is you want the audience to know.

- **Make It Difficult for the Character to Give the Information.** What would do that for you? Maybe she's afraid of his reaction, which will put some tension in the scene and the exposition will then be active.

In "No Fat," Debra has a hard time admitting why her parents are going away for Thanksgiving. There're a lot of relatively unimportant details that go on too long and could be tedious, but when it's done in dialogue, it's more about the emotional dynamic between the couple than simply information. And it's funny, always a bonus.

RAY

How come your parents backed out?

DEBRA

They're going to be out of the
country.

RAY

What? Who leaves America on
Thanksgiving? That's pretty . . .
unthankful.

DEBRA

Don't be so judgmental. They like
to travel and see the world. Just
because your parents never go
farther than . . . here.

RAY

So, where are they goin'?

DEBRA

(very quietly)

They're going to . . . overseas.

RAY

What? What was that?

DEBRA

Nothing. They're going overseas.

RAY

Tell me where.

DEBRA

It's not important. And you don't
need to make fun of them all the
time.

RAY

I won't make fun of them. Where
are they going for Thanksgiving?

```
A LONG PAUSE.

                    DEBRA

          Turkey.
```

- **Give the Character Something Else to Do That's Urgent.** Example: Meredith gives a rundown of medical symptoms to a nurse while stopping blood spurting from a patient's neck wound. The urgency of the situation may help you discover what you don't need to include, and will also give your audience something to be interested in while being fed the exposition. By the way, many of these clunky dialogue problems appear as a result of writing "She tells..." statements in your outline—or did you already figure that one out?

- **Add Character Depth.** Even when you must write highly expositional dialogue in, for example, a *Law & Order* or a *CSI* script, you can give dimension to your characters with just a few words of sharply observed dialogue.

Here is some dialogue taken verbatim from a transcript of an actual deposition regarding an injury lawsuit. The lawyer is pursuing a routine line of questioning with the plaintiff, an elderly woman.

Q: After you fell, were the three workers that were there the first to come to your assistance?
A: Yes.
Q: What kind of shoes were you wearing that day?
A: Boots. Regular ankle boots, Ferragamo.

Ferragamo is an expensive Italian shoe company. In one word we know how important status is to her. A little later in the deposition, the lawyer asks her the following:

Q: Have you ever taken any pictures of the intersection where you fell?
A: No.
Q: Has anybody on your behalf ever taken pictures of the intersection?
A: I was married to a photographer.
Q: Were you?
A: Yes. Very famous all over the world.

Instead of answering the question asked, she takes the opportunity to impress the lawyer again with her status by mentioning her important husband. Then the lawyer questions her about a medical procedure related to the fall:

Q: You continued to experience difficulty in your right shoulder, so you went back to Roosevelt Hospital for another procedure in June, is that correct?
A: Yes. I have two scars to prove it. I had such beautiful shoulders before. I was a model, you know. I haven't been modeling for years.

Her attitude about the scars reveals her vanity. In the course of a few informational questions, we get some revealing backstory and character definition on this woman without a single clunky expositional line.

When you are writing dialogue that has to convey essential facts, add dimension by giving your characters an inner life that is revealed by means of small but telling ways. Your script will feel fresher and more alive.

TOOL BOX

STOP THE EXPOSITION TRUCK

Cover the Information with a Joke.

Give the Character Delivering the Information an Emotional Attitude.

Blend the Information in Later.

Leave It Out.

Make It Now.

Make It Difficult for the Character to Give the Information.

Give the Character Something Else to Do That's Urgent.

Add Character Depth.

Come to Blows

One more thing before you're out of a scene: you need the blow, a.k.a. the button—a line or a reaction that ends the scene with a surprising punch. It doesn't have to be a big punch, but it should feel like punctuation. For a comedy you usually have a good joke to go out on. In a drama the show may use a musical sting to finish it off—an ominous note of tension. Comedies add a funny musical riff. You don't pick the music, you don't even indicate it in your script, but you the writer have to write that joke or moment of suspense. You've got to put the emotional content on the page so the music editor will be able to decide what music to pick later.

Here's the button on Scene "A" of "No Fat."

FRANK GRABS THE BAG.

                    FRANK

          Thank you.

HE STARTS TO GO.

                    MARIE

          Where are you going?

                    FRANK

          On a picnic.

HE GRABS A FORK OFF THE TABLE AND HEADS FOR THE
LIVING ROOM.

                    FRANK (CONT'D)

          (POINTING AT MARIE) Out with the

          old bag. (LIFTING BAG) In with

          the new.

It's a strong joke, but it's not just any joke. It's in character and on story, and a funny summation of the whole scene. It's a great joke and I'd like to take credit for it, but the truth is it was written in a punch-up session by the staff.

Spend time getting your opening scene or sequence in good shape, but don't obsess. Don't try to make it perfect. It's a waste of time and you could get stuck there. After you get through this draft, you will know a lot more about your story and you'll want to bring those discoveries back to bear on your setup.

Once your story is set up, you hang on to your outline like a stair banister and you write! I find it most effective to write this draft fairly fast. You want to get to the end. Some of it will not work, maybe a lot of it. That's okay. That is what a first draft is for. Not to be a finished product, but to show you what doesn't work and get you to the next step.

> **My first TV job,** as you may recall, was writing for *Taxi*. When I turned in my first draft and the rewrite process began, Jim Brooks told me something that has been my guide to writing ever since. I guess he noticed I was in shock (or maybe he just expected me to be), as every beat was taken apart and reassembled. He assured me that this was how it always went and that the purpose of the first draft was to show them what didn't work. That was a life-changing message.

The hard work of writing is the work of preparation. The moment of writing itself—the moment when the thinking work transforms into instinct—may be a nearly effortless flow. You are like the athlete who trains and trains, building strength, honing skills for hundreds of hours, all in preparation for the moment when he needs it. The skater flies across the ice, the batter swings, the boxer punches without thinking about how. This is you now. The exploring, the selecting, the studying of form and the structuring of story is now part of you. You've done your thinking, now you write. You will be surprised by what shows up on the page. Won't that be great!

> You can't think and hit at the same time.
> —YOGI BERRA

14. REWRITING AGAIN, AND AGAIN, AND AGAIN

Sending your script out into the world without rewrites is like sending your six-year-old to school without clothes. You wouldn't think of doing that, so don't do it to your script. You must rewrite. Don't confuse the rewrite process with editing. There is some editing in rewriting, sure, but early rewriting has more to do with reconstructing than with redecorating.

You may be having difficulty finding the trouble spots on your own. Maybe you have a nagging sense that things aren't working but you have no idea why. Show it to people for feedback. If you didn't get professional guidance before, you will most likely want to get some now.

Just as when you got feedback on your outline, you don't expect or even necessarily want solutions. What you do want are signposts indicating where your plot points become illogical or unbelievable, where the action sags, or where the story feels long or uninvolving.

Recognize that you are going to want to argue, explain, and mostly resist almost everything anyone says. It's normal. No writer wants to hear how to improve her script—my God, that means more work! No wonder you don't want to hear it. But listen.

Use the getting-feedback tactics you learned earlier. Take notes. The sheer act of writing it down will keep you from talking.

Take a few days (but not more or you won't want to get back on the horse) to think about what you've heard. Some of the notes will make sense after you've had a chance to relax and actually hear them in the privacy of your own head. The ones you still think are stupid you can dismiss.

ONE EXCEPTION: if you're getting notes from someone who hired you, then no matter how stupid you think the notes are, you do them. If you can take stupid suggestions and make them look good, you will get rehired.

Now tackle your script.

The same tools you used to build story structure in your treatment and outline will be even more useful now that you know more about your story and what your characters do. You may have a new understanding of what your story is about, so adjust your Premise Line.

Your Premise Line shouldn't change completely as in a whole new story. If you change stories now, without working out the problems in this one, you will almost certainly run right into the same kind of problems with the next one. So don't throw everything out. Fix this one. But you can't fix everything at the same time. Focus on one area at a time and let one change lead you to the next.

Earlier techniques discussed for rewriting treatments and outlines will continue to be useful and here are some more tools to add to your rewrite toolkit. Give them all a try so you'll get to know how they work. Don't expect easy answers, and keep asking yourself questions.

What Time Is It?

There is no order to how you use these tools, but I like to start a rewrite by examining the time line because it's concrete and easy to spot.

Do things happen in the appropriate time frame, or have you created a time sequence that defies the laws of physics? Usually time glitches occur in a script because the writer wanted something to happen and just did it without thinking about reality. That's okay for the first draft, but in the rewrite commit to the inconvenience of the real world and adjust your story accordingly. It will make your story easier to follow and it usually makes it more interesting.

Are you taking too much time to show what's happening? Look at your scenes and see if you can move your story faster by eliminating some scenes, or collapsing the action into a single scene.

Say you're writing *The Shield* and you want to show Vic late for work on a day he gets an urgent assignment. You've written a scene that shows him hurriedly leaving his apartment; another one of him rushing to his car; another one of him screeching into a parking space; another one of him greeting co-workers; and another one of him rushing to his desk, where another cop is impatiently waiting for him with an urgent assignment. It conveys what you intended, but it takes too long to get that information. How can you do it faster? Turn five scenes into two: Vic leaves his apartment; he arrives at the station where he's met by another cop, who rushes down the steps, criticizes him for being late, and pulls him into a squad car while ordering him to start a prep for their urgent assignment.

Or even better, do it in one scene: Vic brushes his teeth, when another cop arrives at his apartment to pull him away with the urgent assignment they've been handed. In the next scene you're already moving forward in your story. Vic buttons his shirt in the squad car while the other cop chews him out for being late and a bullet comes through the car window. You've covered all the elements—Vic's late, he's got an urgent assignment, and he's already in danger—you've significantly quickened the pace and your reader is turning the pages!

You wouldn't be able to see the possibility of combining all those elements into one scene without having written it out too long first. That's why you rewrite.

More Set Changes

Now that you know more about your story, rethink your settings. Use the same process you used in picking locations that I described in the outline chapter (Chapter 12). Build tension by setting a scene somewhere unexpected. You may recall a *Raymond* episode in which the family was concerned about an essay one of the kids had written in school, but instead of dealing with it in a scene at home, the writer put the confrontation scene in a priest's office at their church. By taking the family out of the familiar home set, it increased the importance of the problem and made all the characters more tense. The setting upped the stakes and served the story. It was a great choice and the way it intensified the confrontation more than justified the use of an additional set.

What's Up with the Opponent

Examine your "Oh No!" scene carefully. This, after all, is the scene where the point of your story plays out. Is your Central

Character facing off with the most problematic character for her in this story? Have you made that other character a serious contender? Is he formidable enough to make it worth your Central Character's effort?

You want it to be hard for the Central Character; otherwise your story is weak. This is another opportune time to look at your opponent's story as suggested earlier in the Treatment Rewrite tools.

Law & Order SVU did an episode in which Detective Benson confronted her feelings about being a child of rape. The perp in that episode was also a child of rape and his attorney used that as his defense, claiming that he had a predisposition to violence. This gave Detective Benson a strong emotional stake in the case, leading her to question her own reasons for becoming a cop. By creating such a formidable opponent—a character who reflected the most troubling aspects of Benson's own life—the writer was able to dramatize the theme and build a truly meaningful confrontation for Detective Benson.

A common weakness in the confrontation scene is resolving things too easily. Have you avoided some emotional moments? Do you need to step out the action* here? Or do you have the opposite problem? Sometimes the writer has overexplained the emotions. Have you done that? Either too little or too much has the same effect of avoiding the full emotional impact of the moment in dramatic terms. Your character may be crying, you may even be crying, but is your audience? Really, that's who matters.

---

*To step out the action means to take more beats to explore the emotional moment.

Go Back to the Beginning

Now that you know how your big "Oh No!" scene plays out, it's time to go back to your opening scene. You can now sharpen your setup to include appropriate foreshadowing and more motivation. This is a very important step. Very often a problem with the ending needs to be addressed in the setup and you don't know that until you've written your ending.

On-the-Nose Jobs

Got some flat, obvious dialogue? Here's something you can do to liven things up.

Ask yourself, "What response does the character expect when he says this line to another character?" Does he get exactly what he expected? If so, you've discovered why your dialogue is flat or "on the nose." In life we almost never get what we expect, and yet in a script characters almost always do get just what they expect. And that's what gets a "predictable" response from your reader. So change it.

Here's a hypothetical sitcom scene:

```
INT. BEDROOM — DAY

LILY APPLIES EYE MAKEUP. MARSHALL HOPS AROUND
BAREFOOT.

                    MARSHALL

        Where are my socks?
```

> LILY
>
> Right where you left them, in a
>
> wad next to the hamper.

So what do we have? There's attitude: Marshall's frustrated and searching. He asks a question expecting to get the information that will end his search, and Lily answers him with the information he wanted. Let's change it so Lily doesn't give him the convenient answer:

INT. BEDROOM — DAY

LILY APPLIES EYE MAKEUP. MARSHALL HOPS AROUND BAREFOOT.

> MARSHALL
>
> Where are my socks?
>
> LILY
>
> You don't need socks.

Whoa! He wasn't expecting that.

> MARSHALL
>
> Yah, unhuh, I do! This floor is
>
> damn cold.

LILY SNAPS HER MASCARA WAND SHUT AND EXITS. MARSHALL HOPS AROUND AND FINDS A BALLED-UP SOCK NEXT TO THE HAMPER.

Now what have we got? The attitude is sharper and unexpected. Instead of the answer to his question, Marshall got an argument. If I read this, I know there's couple trouble brewing. Great, I'll read on.

When your character gets something he didn't expect, even very small things, it automatically makes him more active. He's thrown off balance, he's got to adjust, he's got to change his tactic. That's emotional action and that is exciting to your audience. When it happens in dozens of small, subtle ways, speech after speech, you've got dialogue that sizzles, from characters who jump off the page.

Try a Lie

In real life, people rarely say exactly what's on their mind. They are doing some form of hiding their real motives and feelings almost all the time. Often they say the opposite of what they mean. And it's not only to other people; very often they are lying to themselves. Ask, "Why would the truth embarrass the character? What emotion is he controlling?" People couch the truth to avoid embarrassment, tweak the truth to shirk responsibility, and cover up the truth to escape blame. They praise people they don't like, they agree to go when they'd rather stay, and they pretend not to know when they know perfectly well. These are all forms of lying, and it's the stuff of genuine human interaction. If you let your characters do some of it, you'll have more engaging dialogue. Watch *The Sopranos* for brilliant examples of characters lying to each other. It's just one of the many things that make the show's dialogue feel so authentic and that series so memorable.

Chronological versus *InternaLogical*

When people talk to each other, they don't necessarily start at
the beginning and proceed in chronological order. It's too neat
and tidy, it's dull. If you've got a long story that your character is
relating, cut to the high point first and then have the character
fill in the pertinent details without rigidly sticking to the
chronology. It will make the speech livelier and probably
shorter.

Avoidance

People often talk about one thing to avoid talking about what's
really on their mind. What are they avoiding? Why? What are
they afraid of? How does it leak out of the edges despite their
best efforts?

Dialogue must carry emotional baggage as well as information. If the dialogue is there because you want the audience to
know something, see if you can find a visual way to communicate the same information. For example, instead of having your
character say an on-the-nose line like:

```
                    MOLLY
          I'm really nervous about meeting
          your mom.
```

Have her actions belie her words:

```
                    MOLLY
          I can't wait to meet your mom.
```

```
MOLLY fusses with the ribbon on the gift box of
chocolates in her lap.
```

We'll get the idea that she's anxious to make a good impression without being told in clunky, expositional words.

Shorthand

You can convey relationships by how much characters leave out of their dialogue when they talk to each other. People who know each other well talk in shorthand. Here's an example of some overwritten dialogue:

```
INT. MAX'S OFFICE — DAY

MAX rifles through the file cabinet. MARLA EN-
TERS, wearing a well-tailored suit that reveals
plenty of cleavage.

          MAX
     Did you pick up the money I told
     you to get from Benson?

          MARLA
     Yes, of course I did, I can get
     anything I want out of that bas-
     tard.

          MAX
     All right! That's great. I knew
     you were the right person to
     send.
```

It sounds kind of stiff, doesn't it? Burdened with too much information and not enough emotion. What if we do this:

INT. MAX'S OFFICE — DAY

MAX rifles through the file cabinet. MARLA EN-
TERS, wearing a well-tailored suit that reveals
plenty of cleavage. She carries an attaché
case.

                    MAX
          So?

MARLA frowns and shrugs. MAX whirls around,
slams his fist into the wall.

                    MAX
          Fuck!

It's a cable network show, apparently.

MARLA slams her case down on the table, pops
the clasps. She grabs a thick wad of bills out
of the case and throws it hard at the back of
MAX's head.

                    MAX
          Hey, what —

MAX whirls around, furious, then sees what hit
him. MARLA smirks.

MAX picks up the wad, jumps on MARLA with a
bear hug, laughing.

                    MAX
          Awright!

With almost no words, the same information is conveyed,
but in a faster, more exciting way and we've got a clearer idea of
their relationship.

Signature Character Lines

Some characters have a line or phrase that they use frequently, and the audience waits for them to say it every show. It's an automatic laugh out of sheer familiarity. But overuse of a signature line is tiresome and a common mistake in spec scripts. If you have a character that has a signature line, do diligent research on how frequently the line appears in scripts; it's almost always less than you think. Use it once—that's enough.

Name Dropping

How often do you use somebody's name in a sentence (when you are speaking to them, not about them)? A lot less than people do in script land. I learned this when I was working for Barry Kemp, the creator and Executive Producer of *Coach*. It really bugged him.

One time somebody (okay, me) wrote something like:

                    LUTHER
          Hayden, where're you going?

                    HAYDEN
          I'm going to look over the game
          films, Luther.

Barry never yelled, but when he saw that, he threw up his hands and said, "They're the only people in the room. They know who they're talking to! The audience knows who they're talking to! Get rid of the names."

Use names judiciously in your dialogue.

Convenient Entrances/Exits

Character entrances need to be motivated; so do the exits. And they need to be motivated from your character's point of view. Wanting a character in a scene to witness something is not a character motive, it's your motive.

It doesn't have to be a big thing, just something to explain why he's there. In "No Fat," my motive for having Ray enter in Scene "A" is that I want him to hear Marie and Frank arguing about their new diet, but that can't be Ray's motive. His motive is that he wants to borrow a garbage bag. We don't even need to know what the garbage bag is for,* but it gives a reason for Ray to enter, plus I got to do a little run about something that personally irks me: people asking to "borrow" something they're not expecting to give back, like Kleenex, or an aspirin.†

Giving your character a reason to enter brings a hint of life going on beyond the confines of the set and adds dimension.

You need to give the same attention to exits. You the writer may not need the character around for the whole scene after she contributed what she was there for, but give that character a motivated reason to leave. Was what just happened embarrassing so she's anxious to get out of there? Is she self-centered and now that she got what she came for she has other, more important things to do? Simple everyday stuff, but include it in the

---

*In an early draft I had him coming in with a rake to borrow a garbage bag to put the leaves in—you know, fall and Thanksgiving. By the time we got to the final draft, that was cut. Too much information. A garbage bag was enough to get him in.

†Page 6 in the script of "No Fat," which you can read on my website (www.SandlerInk.com).

life of the scene. Don't just use a character to do your bidding and then drop him off a cliff.*

This is usually more of an issue with secondary characters, because when your Central Character exits it's generally on a story point. We know where and why he's going, and you'll be picking him up there in the next scene.

Count the Lines

In a television script, dialogue is simple and fast-moving. By counting the lines you'll get an instant readout. Be suspicious of any speeches that go longer than four lines. If you can't trim the speech, break it up with dialogue from another character.

In a few instances, such as the important scene where you're revealing hidden motives, or the Central Character is facing down his opponent, you may have good reason for a lengthy speech, but it better be the Central Character who's got it.

Exercise—Back to the Chart

Now that you have a draft, compare your script with your show samples. Add a column to your research chart and chart your own script. This is like looking in the mirror. You don't go out on an important interview, or a date, or, if you're like me, even

---

*Unless it's part of the action. Cindy Chupack and I wrote a *Coach* episode where Hayden is skiing and he does indeed drop right off a cliff. CUT TO: broken leg.

to the grocery store without checking in the mirror (and probably more than once). I can't think of a quicker way to find out where your script needs work.

If you look at the chart and you see in the script length category the samples run 41, 44, and 40 pages, and your script runs anywhere from 40 to 44 pages, you're in the ballpark. If your script is 45 pages or more, you have a good indication that you have overwritten. You need to go through your script and see what you can condense or cut.

Do you have sections of dialogue or jokes that are off-story? Are characters catching other characters up on what happened in the last scene? Is there a lot of talk about what is going to happen, only to find out that in the next scene, yes, that is exactly what happens? Besides making your script the right length, if you do it with care, cutting will give your script focus, a sharper edge, and a more fluid "read."

If your script is 39 pages or less, don't just add lines. Look for where you've underdeveloped your story. You might do well to check your opposing character for possible further story development, as per our earlier discussion.

Do NOT increase or decrease the margins or font or use any other tricks to manipulate your page count. Cheating your page count only hurts your script. (Yes, of course I've done it. And believe me when I tell you that I just postponed the problem. I inevitably had to go back and fix it or, worse, someone else [my boss] "fixed" it for me.)*

Compare all the items on your chart. Does the "A" scene always run longer than the "B" and "C" scenes? Does yours follow

---

*Okay, if you must, go to my website (www.SandlerInk.com) and you'll find an explanation for how to use your formatting program to discreetly add a line at the end of the page. Promise me you'll only use it once. And never for a whole script!

the pattern? If your "B" scene is longer than your samples, you know that's where you need to go for cuts. Maybe you tried to do too much in the scene, maybe you can move some story action to later or earlier scenes.

If you see that your show has many half-page scenes and you find you have more that run two or three pages, you're off-style. You need to reconfigure how you tell your story so that you conform to the show's pattern.

Does the first scene take place in the same set in all three of your sample scripts? If yours doesn't, you'd better reset your action. How about the second scene? If in your sample scripts one is at the office, one is at a restaurant, and the third is at home, okay, then you've got a choice for your spec.

Look at the Act Breaks. Can you discern a pattern? For example, police procedurals often end Act I with a clue that will lead to the wrong suspect in Act II. If your show does, and your spec doesn't, then you now know you have to restructure.

I know it will be hard, but it will make your script better. An experienced showrunner created this style, and that's a big part of what makes the show work. Take advantage of his expertise and apply it to your spec.

The First Page

Your format must be exact. Follow your script samples. They probably drop down to midpage for the first page, so begin yours in the same place.

Before you send your script out, fine-tune your first page.

If your script is a half-hour comedy, you must have a great joke on page one—a hard joke, not something merely amusing. The first page sets the tone for the entire read. If you're not sure your first joke is good enough, trust your instincts and make it better.

With a drama, make your first page compelling. Don't just show your character getting up in the morning, typical day, etc. Make it somehow special. Here's my favorite example: You know the movie *Bullitt*—yes, it's very old, and if you haven't seen it, rent it, you won't be sorry. Anyway, in *Bullitt*, Steve McQueen lives alone and he doesn't care about or have time for the niceties of life. We know this immediately because he wakes up and goes to make coffee, which we can tell he really needs, but he's out of filters so he digs an old one out of the overflowing garbage, empties the wet grounds, and reuses it. A typical morning scene, but very untypical writing. If there's something like that, small but compelling, on your first page, you can be sure that page is going to get turned. That's your goal.

Do you have to do all these things? No. You don't have to do any of them, but you will have a better script if you do some of them. You certainly aren't going to do all of them for every scene or moment. Use them creatively and do what seems appropriate for your script.

15. THE HEARING TEST

Read It Out Loud

When you have your next draft completed and you feel like you've made progress, it's working, you even like it—that's great! Enjoy it and congratulate yourself. But don't relax completely. It's time for a very big, very scary step. It's not dangerous, but it is terrifying. Now you have to hear it read OUT LOUD. In front of people. Anywhere is fine; your living room will do.

It doesn't matter so much who reads it or who hears it. It's the actual doing that's important. If you know some actors—they don't have to be the right type for the role, though generally I like to stay within gender and age range boundaries—invite them over to read your script. Almost all the actors I know are eager to perform and are most generous with their time. If you don't know any actors, you can ask anyone who isn't too shy to speak in public. I've heard many scripts read aloud by writers, nonactors if ever there were any, and it's perfectly sufficient for this purpose.

This reading is for you and maybe a couple of selected friends and fellow writers to listen to your script. What this most definitely is NOT NOT NOT is a reading for someone who you think can help you with your career. No agents, producers, managers; no one very important whom you hope to impress. This is not a backer's audition or a promotional tool of any kind. This is a writer's tool. A big one, a very important one, but it is strictly a developmental step in your writing process. This is public, but it is not a performance. If you attach the burden of performance to this reading you will sabotage the intended purpose, which is to illuminate the areas that still need work.

Nothing else identifies useless deadwood faster than hearing your script read out loud in front of people. Doesn't matter which people, doesn't even matter how many, could be only one besides you. The painful truth is unavoidable in a reading. You will hear what lines are too "written" or unnecessary, what jokes aren't funny, which speeches go on too long. It will be crystal clear. Painfully so. But that's what you want to know. That's why you don't invite "important people."

You'll also hear a lot of things that don't quite follow logically; you'll hear where characters make a clumsy transition, where they don't work hard enough to get what they want, where supporting characters have not been given sufficient action or motive.

Please don't read a role yourself. If you don't have enough actors for all the roles, it's fine if they double up. Read all the roles out loud as much as you want when you're writing, but for this reading give yourself the benefit of having nothing to do but listen and notate in your script where things are off, or, just as important, where they are on.

Be sure to assign someone to read descriptions of action, again not you. You need to listen. It could be an actor who is

THE HEARING TEST   159

also reading a small role. Instruct this reader to read the slug lines (but not the list of characters in parentheses below the slug line in a multi-camera script). This reader reads aloud the stage directions such as entrances and exits but not the parentheticals. Those are the descriptions in parentheses just under the name of a character that suggest how the actor should read the line, e.g., (WHISPERS). And by the way, the fewer of those descriptions you include in your script the better. Go over these instructions with all the actors present so they will know which directions they should pause for and which they should read through.

You don't need to have a rehearsal. It's not about performance. In fact, a great performance will actually be a disservice to you. You want to hear how the words play without the benefit of funny, wonderful actors who are just perfect for the part.

This spec script is going to be read by agents' assistants, producers' development staff, and so forth. They will not be hearing that great performance in their heads. All they will have are your words. So that's all you need to concern yourself with at this reading.

Give your readers a copy of the script in advance so they can get familiar with it on their own. Give each actor a clean and *complete* copy of the script, even if they're only in one scene. They will probably want to highlight their speeches and also have a sense of when they appear in relationship to the whole.

Arrange chairs in a semicircle for the actors so they can see each other when speaking. Seat the Central Character in the center and the supporting cast in order of importance on either side.

Arrange seating for the audience; everyone should be able to see and each person should have a seat. Borrow (or rent) folding chairs if you need extra seating.

Before the reading starts, the only direction you should give your actors is to read the words exactly as they are written. Instruct them to please not add any words or leave any out. You want to hear it exactly as you have written it, for better or worse. Ask them to please read loudly and quickly but without rushing. If an actor has questions about pronunciation or meaning, of course, answer them. Reassure them that however they choose to interpret the lines will be fine. Any other direction is irrelevant and inappropriate. Let everyone know that this is not a performance so much as an opportunity for you to hear where the problems are in the script.

After the reading, thank your readers profusely. I don't care what you thought of their reading. If you are like most writers, you will have hated at least one of them. Never, never, never blame the readers, or the audience for that matter. Believe me, it will be tempting, but resist. It's your words, and only your words, that you should be concerned with. If a reader stumbled or gave an interpretation that wasn't how you would have liked it, that doesn't matter. Remind yourself that your script is going to be read by lots of people and you will not be able to control their interpretations and the inflections in their head as they read it. If something didn't work, you, the writer, take responsibility for it.

Put out the munchies and invite comments. Include the actors in the discussion. They will have a unique perspective on your characters and often have interesting and valuable contributions.

Now comes the hardest part for you. You must discipline yourself to LISTEN. Simply listen. No excuses. No explanations. No justifying anything. You have only a short time for everyone's full attention on your material. Don't use it up talking. You already know what you think. As with all the other times you got feedback, make lots of notes to help curtail your urge to speak.

At the end, thank everyone—actors and audience—again. Even if you're in shock, you're not allowed to overlook this. It may have been painful for you, but they have helped you more than you can say.

> **Never complain,** never explain. No one's listening anyway, it's all just noise.
>
> —GROUCHO MARX

To Record or Not to Record

Some writers want to record the reading. You can, if the actors don't mind (be sure to ask them for permission; it's polite and respectful of their craft). However, I don't think recording is a useful thing to do. I believe you will get the greatest benefit by focused listening while it's happening. The audience listening with you is key, and you won't have that element later if you're listening to the recording by yourself. It loses something valuable.

I also believe that if you think you will have it to listen to again later, you will listen less attentively when it's happening.

If you still feel you want to record the reading, ask a friend to handle it for you. Even though it's simple, you will be in a high emotional state; you don't need one more thing to do.

TOOL BOX

FIRST DRAFT READING CHECKLIST

Ask actors to read.

Ask friends to attend.

Assign roles, double up if necessary.

Assign someone to read stage directions and descriptions.

Send actors scripts in advance, but do not rehearse.

Arrange the room.

Provide snacks and beverages.

Listen to feedback.

Thank everyone. Very important.

Yes, Again

After you have recovered from the reading, you know what you have to do. That's right. Rewrite, based on what you heard. Not just what others told you they heard, although that will certainly be something you will want to consider, but what you yourself heard.

Do not stop now. Keep writing. There is nothing wrong in deciding that you don't want to write, but decide that after you have finished, not when you're in the middle of rewrites.

16. FINAL POLISH

When your script works. Really works. When the feedback you get is enthusiastic, and you can tell that people aren't just being polite; they really "get it." Put the script down, get away from it for at least 24 hours. Do anything else. Or nothing else, but don't concern yourself with your script. It needs to breathe, like fine wine. And you need to get some perspective.

When you come back to your script, read it. Just read it. Make check marks and brief reminder notes if something strikes you as weak or long, but don't do anything about it yet. Like the lines in the Cluster Exercise, the notes are there to keep you on the page and connected. Personally, I like to do this part of the process with a blue pencil on a printed copy of the script. I think it's quicker and easier to make marks on a page than on the computer, and the blue pencil is my own little editing ritual.

Now you can invite that noisy editor in your head, the one we banished long ago in the exploration phase. Now we need her. Go over your script again. Look at the places you've marked. See if you can identify what it is that's bothering you. If you can name the problem, you will be able to fix it. Don't worry if you can't identify everything. Just start with what you *can* name.

Cutting Remarks

Find anything you can cut. Lines that can go. Things you may be saying twice. Look in your stage directions and descriptions. There are always extra words hiding out there. Find quicker, smoother ways of conveying your information. Sentence fragments are okay in the descriptions. Cutting even one word can make a difference. You don't want a single thing to slow down the read. Think of Olympic swimmers—they shave their entire bodies because they can't afford to lose the one-hundredth of a second that body hair pulling through the water would cost them. Consider Hollywood as competitive as the Olympics.

> If it can be cut, do.
> —GEORGE S. KAUFMAN, PULITZER PRIZE–WINNING
> DRAMATIST AND THEATER DIRECTOR

Punch Up

If you've written a comedy, look at every joke. Are you sure you haven't heard that one or something dangerously close to it before? Don't cut it, because your instinct is probably right, there should be a joke there, but make it a better joke. If you can't think of a better joke, mark the spot and we'll get back to this.

There may be sections in your script where you've gone too long without a joke. Mark those spots too.

> **I use the letters JTK**—to indicate "Joke to come." Why "K" instead of "C"? Because in Neil Simon's *The Sunshine Boys,* the characters, two old vaudeville comics, argue about what words are funny. One insists to the other, "Words with a 'K' are funny." Neil Simon is a pretty funny writer; I figure he knows something.

You may have a section in your big scene where things get serious, and you don't want to interrupt the emotional impact with a joke every two lines. But if you do have a serious moment, you want to make sure you cut the tension with a joke after you've made your point.

If your script is a drama you can still use some humor. Not the kind of jokes that a sitcom uses, but the cops on *Law & Order* make jokes, the lawyers on *Boston Legal* have a dry sense of humor, doctors on TV seem to be required to have a macabre sense of humor. So let your characters see the humor in frustrating situations, have a laugh on themselves, or better yet, get the best of an opponent with a laugh. Some comedy can liven up a dramatic script and make it a much better read.

Okay, let's go back to those marks you made in the script where you know there should be more or better humor. This is where you need to have friends. Get together with a couple of other writers whom you like and think are funny.* Go through

---

*A group is most fun, but you can do it one-on-one.

your script and stop at all those places where you noted JTK (or whatever code you want to use). Brainstorm. Don't just look at the punch lines; often the fix is in the setup. Use the Count to 10 Exercise to come up with unexpected images, setups, ideas, and lines that can improve your joke. Create an atmosphere of possibility—you'll go through a lot of bad jokes to find a good one.

This is not cheating, this is a legitimate comedy tool. On every sitcom, a whole lot of jokes go into the script at the table. Comedy happens when people are working off each other, topping each other, building and taking off each other.

This is the fun part. When you say, "I write sitcoms" and people say, "Oh, that must be fun," this is the part they're thinking of. You slaved to get your story, you invested countless hours to get character-driven humor in every scene. Now that it works, the house is done, you get to hang pictures and throw brightly colored pillows around. So have some fun and get the best comedy you can into your script.

17. LOOKS MATTER

It's Hollywood, baby, appearance is everything. You've done the hard stuff if you've written a great script. Now be sure it looks the part. The script must be done to industry standards if you expect it to be considered in the professional marketplace. Since you have written all your drafts in correct format, you now only need to double-check all the elements to be sure that none have been accidentally missed. Computers have their own peculiar logic and details like all caps and the proper line spacing can get overlooked when you revise, cut, and paste. Correct any widows,* or anything else that doesn't look exactly like your show's script.

Please ensure that all character names are correct. Is this too dumb to have to tell you? Well, maybe, but I promise you, I've seen a number of scripts with character names misspelled. My guess is that these are specs from writers who have only watched the show on TV. You have to look at the script to know

---

*Single lines at the bottom of pages. See Showbiz Meanings of Regular Words: A Selective Glossary for more.

that it's "Carin" not Karen, "Danny" not Dani, "Britney" not Brittany. (True confessions: I once misspelled "Ally" on an *ELR* script—I think I spelled it "Alley." Ray noticed! Oh my God!)

I'm sure I don't have to tell you this one, but I'm going to anyway because I've seen it more than once. *NO* handwritten corrections, additions, or anything on the pages of any script you send out.* Your pages must be pristine. Handwritten notes will stop a reader in her tracks. It's so unprofessional, it could very well get your script instantly dumped in the DNR† pile.

You must also proofread for typos, spelling, and punctuation. Once is not enough. Your computer's spell-check is a good start, but it is also not enough. It doesn't know the difference between "your" and "you're" or "there," "their," and "they're."

You must make sure you use those words and all words correctly. You are a writer. Words are your business. Words are also a professional reader's business, and there is a very good chance yours will have gone to a top-tier college and knows correct usage. It doesn't necessarily knock you out of the ball game to get a word wrong, but it certainly doesn't help you.

I am not a good proofreader: first of all, I'm a bad speller, so I often don't know when a word is wrong. Second, I get sucked into the story all the time, completely losing track of what I'm supposed to be looking for. And third (you knew there'd be three), I am an obsessive tinkerer; I can't leave words and lines alone, so I get distracted. A trick that someone told me is to proofread your script backward. That does help keep me from getting caught up in the story, but it does nothing for my spelling.

After I proof my final draft as many times as I can stand, I have

---

*If you're taking feedback notes, of course, you can write all over the pages; that's for your personal use. Just don't write anything on something you give to someone else.

†Hospital code for Do Not Resuscitate. I use it to mean Don't Need to Read.

to get help from better eyes than mine. I ask my friends and loved ones. But even if it means you have to pay a professional proof-reader, don't send out a script with typos and/or misspelled words.

The Title Page

First of all, never send out work without a title page. If you are sending a script as an email attachment, be sure you choose the option that includes your title page. Most programs won't do this automatically, you have to tell it to.

There are some big pitfalls on the title page, and you can mark yourself as an amateur before your reader even gets to page one! The good news is, there are clear and simple rules, and all you have to do is follow them.

For your title page you do not copy the style of the production scripts that you have been using for your research.

A spec script title page should have the name of the show in all caps, the title of your episode in quotes, your writer's credit indicated as "written by." Don't use story and teleplay by, don't use conceived by—use written by, followed by your name on the next line.

If you wrote the script with a partner, you decide who goes first by any means you like, and use an ampersand (&) to separate your names. You do not use the word "and" to indicate a partnership. In film and television the word "and" in the writing credits indicates that a new writer was brought in to rewrite you. This would never be an appropriate credit on a spec script.

The only other information on your title page is your contact information or, if you have an agent or manager, their name and contact information. That's all.

It should lay out on the page like this:

```
SHOW NAME

"Episode Title"

written by

Your Name (& Your Partner's Name)




                                              Contact:
                          Your Name (& Your Partner's Name)
                                      Your phone number
                                      Your email address
```

Use the same white paper for your title page that you use for your script. You can use a heavier-grade card stock if you really want to but it is not necessary or expected. If you do use card stock, use white, no colors. No pictures or drawings even if they did it on the show script. No pictures, graphs, charts, or maps anywhere in your script.

And no fancy fonts. Use the same typeface on the title page that you use for your script, `Courier 12 point`. If the script you've been reading is a shooting script, it will most likely have a title page that uses the show's logo font for the name of the show. Do NOT use the show's logo font on your spec script. I know you're dying to scan it into your computer and use it, but it is under copyright and it is not yours to use. It can also be misinterpreted. You may think you are being professional, but the reader may think you're presumptuous, or, worse, that you are trying to pass off a spec script as a produced credit.

Speaking of copyright, did you notice that nowhere on the title page did I indicate a copyright? That is not an oversight. Do not put copyright information on the title page of your spec script (or anywhere on your spec). DO copyright your material, absolutely,* just don't write it on your title page. If you are dealing with professionals, it is assumed that you have had your work copyrighted. By announcing that you have obtained a copyright, you look amateurish. I know the studio has one with a big warning on the title page of the production script you've been using as a bible, but that's the studio, their legal department insists.† It doesn't belong on your spec.

Your show script may have a date and a draft ID # on it, but

---

*See Chapter 27 for copyright options.

†I was shocked when I signed my first contract and saw the clause that says the studio is the author! They become the author so that they hold the copyright. You do not own the scripts you write when you are paid to write them for a studio.

your spec should not. You can date your own personal copies if you like, in order to keep track of your drafts, but there is no reason or benefit to date the scripts you send out. People in Hollywood want to read what's hot off the printer. A date will make your script, well, dated. Leave it off. You also don't put anything like First Draft, Second Draft.

So few words on the page and yet so much that can go wrong...

Numbers

Professional software programs number correctly for you. If you aren't using a professional program, you'll need to be aware of the following conventions (and even if you've used the software, pay attention to your show's protocols): Your title page does not have a number. Your first page of dialogue is page 1, but generally the numbers start with 2 on your second page. I always start numbering at 2, but I have noticed that some production scripts start on 1. I think you can do either. Numbers on scripts go in the upper-right-hand corner. I have seen some scripts with the numbers centered, but standard form is upper right; stick with that.

Paper

Standard white, 20- or 24-pound office paper. Three-hole punch. No exceptions.

Binding

No clips, no staples, no Velobind, no spiral binding, no spring binders, no three-ring notebooks, or any other form of binding is acceptable for a television spec script. Do not put your script in a folder or a plastic cover of any kind.

Use only Acco $1^1/_4''$ solid brass brads.* Do not use longer ones; they catch on readers' clothing, cut their fingers, and are generally a nuisance. Do not use the thin, flimsy brads you find at most Kinko's or Office Depots either; they're terrible and fall out.† Don't burden a reader with putting your script back together after it falls all over his floor.

Use only the top hole and bottom hole. Leave the middle hole empty. This is a must. Put three brads in a TV script and you're marked as an amateur immediately.

Why only two? Because on a show in production, scripts are rewritten on a daily basis—sometimes even more than once a day. There are over a hundred people who work on a show, and every one of them needs an updated script. One less brad makes a big difference to the writer's assistants and the P.A.s†† who have to open up 100 scripts and stick in the new pages. Even though your script is not going out to a crew, two brads is the standard, so that's the way you want to do it.

I've repeated over and over that you must use your research scripts as a guide; however, the scripts you've been studying are most likely shooting scripts and there are some details in shooting scripts that you should definitely NOT include in your spec.

---

*Order them online from the Writers Store (see Appendix III: Sources).
†I'm told that some Kinko's located near studios in Burbank have the proper brads.
††Production Assistants

You should not put in any camera directions. In a multi-camera show you may see RE SET at the end of a scene. That is a camera direction. It's there only for production purposes. All you need is your slug line at the top of the new scene. It is also unnecessary for you to include DISSOLVE TO: or CUT TO: or any other editing indications at the end of scenes. They're fun, I know, and writers used to include those directions, but for ease and speed of reading, they are being left out in more and more scripts, especially single-camera format. You will actually look more in the know if you leave them out. There are instances where you want to use a scene transition indicator for emphasis, but in general I think you should leave them out.

A production script will have a heading at the top of every page with the name of the show, the episode, the draft, the date, the page number, and, if it's a multi-camera show, an Act number and a scene letter. However, none of that except the page number belongs in your spec script.

There may also be some extra pages at the beginning of your research script, a cast list, a set list, a rehearsal schedule, and/or a couple of pages of scene breakdowns, called a Short Rundown. None of these pages should appear in your spec script. Those are for production drafts only. A staff writer turns in what is called a Writer's Draft. None of these various production pages are in that draft, and they don't belong in yours either.

You may also notice in a production draft that the slug line has an item that appears in parentheses as DAY or NIGHT followed by a number. It will look like this: INT. LIVING ROOM − DAY (DAY 1). That's for the wardrobe department, so they can track how many costume changes there are going to be. Your slug lines should simply say INT. LIVING ROOM − DAY and not include the additional (DAY 1).

18. I'VE PUT THIS OFF LONG ENOUGH

> If you are not scared you are not writing.
> —ANNIE DILLARD, *THE WRITING LIFE*

I've been procrastinating writing about how to combat procrastination.

If you were a purely creative artist you could wait for your moment of inspiration, but you are writing a TV script and, therefore, you are a commercial artist. You must be able to access your talent whenever you need it, which means you need to control the circumstances that set your creative flow in motion. I'm an expert at procrastination—I'll bathe the dog, make eggplant parmigiana from scratch, even go to the dentist, to avoid writing—so I have had to create many techniques to get myself to the desk. And I've needed all of them.

Tools to Combat Procrastination

A deadline

Money is the most persuasive motivator I know; consequently the best deadline is the one with a check at the end of it. But what about when you're doing your own work? You've got to create deadlines for yourself.

Give yourself a reason why your treatment or your draft must be done by a certain date. It could be that you want to submit to a contest, or you want to finish a draft before you go on vacation. You can join a writer's group and commit to having a scene done by the meeting date. Whatever date you set for yourself, make it a commitment.

Give yourself small goals

Really small goals. I often ramp up the writing process by doing a bit of editing on the previous day's work. It eases me in almost without realizing I'm in the pool. The water doesn't feel as cold. "Today, I'll check the spelling on the scene I wrote yesterday." No problem, I can do that.

If your goal is to write a script, that's going to be overwhelming. All you'll see is how much you still have to do. Plan to do one small thing and then do it. The smaller the task, the more likely you'll complete it. Accomplishing one small thing gives you momentum—you did what you set out to do. Allow yourself to enjoy the accomplishment. Recognize your accomplishment and reward yourself. I like chocolate, myself.

Once you do one thing, it's easier to go on and do another. If you finished checking the spelling, set a goal of writing the description of the next scene's location. Just that. Nothing more. It may only be one sentence. That's fine. Set the next goal: write the opening action. You may take off and write the whole scene this way. Great. Tomorrow you'll have another scene to check for spelling.

Scheduling

Make a commitment to your deadlines and goals by putting your writing time on your calendar. If you write it down, you are emphasizing your commitment to it, visually, physically, and psychically. If it's written on your calendar, when other things come up, you'll be more likely to schedule them around your writing time. If an emergency comes up, reschedule your writing time just like you would any other appointment.

If it's not in writing, it's too easy for your time to disappear into the mist of the distractions of life. I have the lost days to prove it.

Involve another person

I often work with partners and having to keep an appointment with them makes me get to work when, if I were alone, I'd probably be napping. When I know that someone is expecting me to show up with pages, I do. It's too humiliating not to.

Many of my clients use weekly coaching appointments this way. They know I'm going to call in a week to review a specific section of work and since they pay for my time, it would be a real waste not to be ready.

Change "I should" to "I want"

Get the word "should," as in "I should write that scene today," out of your vocabulary. Change "should" to "want." "I want to write that scene today."

Words have power—if you're a writer, you must believe that—and when you change the word, you change your attitude. By getting rid of "should" you've eliminated the implied authority figure and, therefore, you've eliminated the need to rebel against it. The writing is no longer a burden that you feel obligated to do. You *want* to do it. It's your choice and the resistance is minimized.

Rituals

Getting a cup of coffee in the same cup; sharpening six pencils; cleaning your desk (careful with that one, it can lead to cleaning the bookshelves, and then the books, and then the pictures and, oh my God, it's 4:30 PM . . . or AM)—anything that you do the same way every time before you sit down to work that creates a habit. Connect that cup of coffee with going to the keyboard and after a while you won't even have to tell yourself to do it. The habit does it for you. I'm sure you've tried to break a bad habit, and you know how hard it is. A good habit can harness that same strength and become a powerful tool to help you accomplish your goal.

> A professional is a person who can do his best at a time when he doesn't particularly feel like it.
> —ALISTAIR COOKE, BBC JOURNALIST

Consistency

The more frequent your writing times, the better. One hour every day is far better than six hours once in a while. Ninety minutes every other day is better than four hours on an occasional weekend. You'll get much more done because you know you have limited time. With only an hour or two, you won't have time for breaks to use the phone or to plan your TV viewing. It's the habit thing again. If you can schedule your work for the same time every day, it will be even better.

Icons

If you believe in magic, give yourself some "magic" props. Designate a writing shirt, have a "lucky pen," or put a Writing Goddess on your desk. Personally, this stuff just annoys me, but for some people it works.

Give yourself permission to write badly

"If you try to be perfect, you'll end up being less than good." My son said this to me when he was eight years old, and I had him write it down for me in his little-boy scrawl. Thirteen years later, I still have that up on the bulletin board in my office. Famous people may have said similar things in more grandiose terms, but I love his simple version.

Demanding that what you write be good is only good for stopping you. Permission to write badly will free you to put something on the page. Anything on the page is progress. Risk writing badly; it just might come out good despite your lack of confidence.

Stay in the chair

One more technique. This one's foolproof.

Every bit of writing depends on your ability to stay in the chair. As long as you are physically in the chair, you will eventually write something. The second you get up, you're done. So when you feel the urge to get up (oh, you'll feel it—it's hardwired in, fight or flight, you know), breathe and stay there just thirty seconds more. There's a good chance if you get past the impulse (a.k.a. fear) you'll find the courage to write something. You can fix something that doesn't work if it's on the page. You can do nothing with something brilliant in your head.

If none of these tactics keeps you at your desk, you can try what Victor Hugo, the great French author, did when he felt the urge to hang out in cafés. Have your servant take away all your clothes and not bring them back until you're finished writing for the day.

> **I've got** a solid brass pencil shaped paperweight on my desk and engraved on it is: "If you want to write, write." That is the whole point of this book, summed up in one sentence.

PART III

What You Need to Know Now That You Have a Script

19. THE PITCH

> Every idea you present must be something you could get across easily at a cocktail party with strangers.
>
> —JACK WELCH, CEO OF GENERAL ELECTRIC

Pitching. A sometimes exhilarating, but often scary experience in which you present your ideas verbally to a potential buyer, either face-to-face or on the phone. In other words, it's talking. Most writers became writers to AVOID talking. But verbal pitching is a reality in Hollywood and particularly in television.

If your spec script is great, it will do what it's supposed to do: get TV producers interested in you as a writer. When that happens, you are going to be pitching. A good pitch turns into an assignment. And an assignment . . . well, you know what an assignment turns into: **$!** Finally, I have a formula for you: **SS+P=$.*** It's not **SS=$.** Without the **P** you don't get the **$.** So clearly, if you want to do what you love and get paid for it, you are going to have to pitch.

There are some people who are great at pitching. I have known a couple and have watched in awe as they effortlessly regale their audience. They have a wonderful time in meetings

---

*SS stands for Spec Script, P stands for Pitch, and $—I don't have to tell you.

and then fall apart when they have to actually write what they've sold—or so I like to think.

Personally, I find pitching my ideas to development executives, studio people, producers, even other writers, at the very least intimidating and often terrifying, but I have found that there are ways to, if not thoroughly enjoy the pitching process, at least get comfortable with it. I tell you this so you will know that there is hope. And also so you will know that each and every tip I have for you has been personally tested by me in actual combat.

Short Is Better

Keep it short. Thirty seconds is an eon in a story pitch. Whoever is listening to your pitches does not want to spend her time trying to find your idea through a tsunami of details. Getting your story into a clear, concise form shows respect for her time and intelligence. Your purpose in pitching is not to tell the whole story, but rather to tell your listener the *idea* of the story so that she will want to read your carefully written script.

A concise pitch also shows respect for your own work. Vague, lengthy descriptions with an excess of details betray a lack of preparation, as well as a lack of confidence in your own idea. Make the effort to distill your pitch down to a few cogent sentences and you will be respected as a professional.

Unless It's *Too* Short

A frequent mistake: A writer will pitch an interesting setup— and that's all. A setup, no matter how funny or interesting, is not a story. The story is what happens as a *consequence* of the setup and a good pitch must include that.

> **When I pitched the story** that would become "No Fat" to Phil Rosenthal, the Executive Producer, the setup was Marie goes on a diet to lose weight, but the story is about the consequence of that: i.e., what happens to Ray when she doesn't cook what he's used to. The way he relates to his mom is through food. If she's not feeding him, how is he going to relate to her? How is anybody in the family going to relate to her? Are they even a family without Marie's cooking?
>
> Phil didn't like the idea of Marie on a diet to lose weight, but he did like the idea of what would happen to Ray and the family if Marie's cooking changed. Since the diet was just the setup, that was easy to change. Phil said make it Frank and make it for health reasons. Thus it was so, and I had an episode assignment.

What's in a Pitch

Your pitch should include:

- The Setup
- What your Central Character wants, and who's in the way of his getting it
- What's the risk and the Turning Point—two Turning Points if you know them

Use the same tools to find your pitch ideas that you used to find your spec script story. Create a Pitch Line the same way you created a Premise Line. You don't have to develop a complete story treatment or even a beat sheet. You just need the idea and some specifics—not the details.

Remember the synopsis you wrote? The synopsis is a good guide to how much material you ought to have for a pitch. See Chapter 6 if you'd like to review. You can also review the discussion on the differences between details and specifics there. However, you may find that you have to develop a lot of details before you can simplify your story down to a short version. That's okay, just don't include all that stuff in your pitch. Somebody once told me when I was learning to pitch, that the more you include the more they have to object to. After hearing a thousand pitches, I can verify that.

■ Why you want to tell it

Your passion for the story. You don't necessarily have to say it directly in your pitch, although a suggestion of your personal connection can sometimes be effective. If you're comfortable mentioning where the idea came from go ahead, but make it brief—as in one sentence—don't go into a lot of personal detail with an involved anecdote about your life.

Practice

The key to a confident pitch is practice. Practice your pitch over and over and over, *but*—and this is important—don't make it letter-perfect. Do not memorize it. *A memorized pitch is a dead pitch.*

What if the person you're pitching to gets excited about something you say and asks a question? If you're on a memorized track, you will be thrown off. You want to be comfortable and completely familiar with your pitch material, but also free to improvise if appropriate.

Your real purpose in pitching is to connect with the person you're pitching to. You want to engage the imagination of your listener so she can see how your story could work for her.

Even worse than memorizing is reading a pitch. I know the security blanket aspect is tempting, but it's too formal, too "written." If a pitch was just what was written down on paper, you could email your list of story ideas to producers and showrunners and they could pick one. It would save everybody a lot of time and pain. But that's not what a pitch is. A pitch is your story *plus* your personality and passion. If you've memorized your pitch or are reading your pitch, the doors are closed; you are not open for business.

Exception: If you're pitching a bunch of ideas, it's okay to have a list of titles or key words for reference.

One time I had a pitch meeting that I hadn't had much time to prepare for. I hadn't practiced my pitch on anybody, so while I was in the studio lobby waiting to be called in to the meeting, I asked an actress who was waiting for an audition if she would do me a favor and listen to my pitch. It was actually harder to get up the nerve to ask her to listen to me than it was to pitch it. As soon as I started the pitch, I felt better. She laughed in the right places and said she liked it. Maybe she just wanted to be nice because she thought I could give her a job someday, whatever. I went into that meeting feeling a whole lot more confident. I don't know how her audition went, but I sold my idea.

Practice working a pitch into conversations with friends, your friends' friends, the person at the next table in Starbucks, anyone who will listen. Practice making eye contact and making the listener a part of the give-and-take. Adjust your pitch and tweak it each time you pitch it, using what you learned from the last time.

You want to be so familiar with the story that you don't have to think about the words you use. You want to connect with the idea and then tell your story, just as if it were a conversation. An animated, exciting, lively conversation.

You've seen actors on talk shows promoting their new movie or their new TV series. They may appear to be just talkin' with Dave or Jay, but in fact they and their material are well prepared. Stars know exactly what points to hit. If you see the same actors on multiple shows, you'll start to notice that the casual chat and clever "ad-libs" have a familiar sound. Some actors are more skilled than others at disguising the preparation, but you can definitely hear the script in their patter. They are improvising around the prepared material and they do it in a way that feels relaxed and natural. That's the way you want to pitch.

You're not an actor? Take an acting class or, even better, an improv class—it will help you gain presence when you're "on." I worked with a highly talented writer who was charming, funny, and very socially outgoing, but when she was first starting out she was intimidated by pitching. She took a stand-up comedy workshop, not because she had a secret desire to go on the road with her jokes, but to give her some tools for pitching. I think it worked, because she's sold a bunch of stories and pilots over the years.

No Reviews—Good or Bad

Pitching is selling, but nobody likes to be sold to. Beware of over-selling your material. When I hear people preface a pitch with good reviews like, "This is a really funny story," or "This one's great, you'll love it," I usually miss the first sentence of the actual pitch because I'm busy thinking, "Oh yeah? Really? I'll love it? We'll see." You will appear more confident and the idea will come across stronger without you pumping it up beforehand.

On the other hand, please no bad reviews either: "This is probably a terrible idea. . . ." "You've probably already got this. . . ." "I haven't really worked this one out yet, but . . ." If you feel you have to apologize for the idea, why are you pitching it?

Apologizing for your work may make you feel more comfortable, but it is not professional. Taking responsibility for your work and doing your best is. Make the effort to prepare and then pitch what you've got with commitment and without comment.

Listening

It's harder than you think, and more important than you can imagine.

> Most people do not listen with an intent to understand.
> Most people listen with an intent to reply.
> STEPHEN COVEY, AUTHOR OF
> *THE 7 HABITS OF HIGHLY EFFECTIVE PEOPLE*

In order to connect with the people you're pitching to, you want to listen for cues so you can identify what the opportunities might be. Listen actively to catch attitudes, interests, needs, and areas of commonality. You've got to be constantly taking the temperature of the room. This skill may not come easily to you, but here are some exercises that will sharpen your listening skills.

Exercises—Zen and Groucho

If you're home alone, practice . . .

Zen (the sound of one hand clapping)

Choose a particular sound like birdsongs, pet noises, furnace sounds, traffic, anything. The sound is not so important; whatever amuses you is fine. Set your timer for one minute and listen for that particular sound. That's all. Listen and see if you hear that sound in that one minute of time that you set aside for focused listening.*

If you're in a social situation, experiment with . . .

Groucho (say the secret word)

Choose a particular word and listen for it. It can be a common word like "good," or relatively uncommon like "burn." It could even be rare like "penultimate," though that's probably going to reduce your ability to stay interested in the exercise. Again, it doesn't matter what the word is. Give yourself five minutes to listen for that word.

Keep track of the number of times you hear it. That's it, that's all you do. Mark crosshatches on a sticky note or keep count on

---

*This is related to meditation and may have some anti-stress benefits as well. This claim is completely unsubstantiated by any clinical research; I'm just saying it works for me.

your fingers. It doesn't matter if you hear it seven times or none. Either way you will be listening with purpose. The idea is the *experience* of focused listening, not the result.

Are you thinking that if you do this in conversation it's going to make you seem vaguely distracted? Quite the opposite. You know how people like to hold a glass so they have something to do with their hands? This is the mental equivalent; it gives you something to do with your ego. Focused listening will slow down your need to talk about yourself; consequently, you'll hear more of what the other person is saying, you'll ask more relevant questions, and they, in turn, will find you scintillating. (See "Stop talking" in the next chapter.)

But how will this really help you? Like physical exercises, doing them once won't do much. It's the repetition that builds strength and makes these listening exercises effective. Lifting weights isn't about being more proficient at lifting objects as much as it's about building muscle mass. You're building a creative muscle. Repeating listening exercises will make you more alert and increase your awareness. It will also give you practice in tuning in to what is being said and that will be a valuable skill in any pitching, note-taking, or contact-making situation.

The Meeting

If you've been asked to come in to meet a showrunner, even if your agent or the assistant who set up the meeting said it's just a meet and greet, be prepared to pitch something. If they like you, they'll probably ask if you have any ideas. In fact, if you're not asked to pitch, offer to. Why wouldn't you want to make the most of the opportunity of being in a room with a showrunner? Come prepared and don't be shy about offering ideas.

TOOL BOX

MEETINGS

You'll be offered something to drink and you'll need it, because when you pitch you're going to be nervous and that means your mouth is going to get dry.

Take water—don't ask for coffee: it's hot, it's complicated (What do you take with it, milk? Whole milk, skim milk, 2 percent milk? Sugar, sugar substitute?). Even if you don't care, the assistant whose job it is to get it for you has been trained to ask, so just don't get into it.

Then there's the caffeine; you don't need any extra stimulant. If the thought of pitching hasn't gotten enough adrenaline going, you're just dead.

Herbal tea? Seems like a good choice, nice and soothing. No. You will have to deal with the dripping tea bag when you extract it and you will have to extract it to drink it, or risk having the bag fall on your face. (Okay, don't ask me how I know this, just believe me, it will happen.)

But if these reasons are not convincing enough, remember you're nervous, you're on unfamiliar territory, there's a real likelihood of spilling. Coffee or tea will leave stains; so will soda and it's sticky. You want to be remembered, but not as "oh yeah, the writer who left that icky residue on my glass top table" or "the writer who left that tea stain on my suede sofa."

Just take the bottled water. Oh, and don't bring your own. It telegraphs that you don't know the rituals. You will *always* be offered something to drink at a Hollywood meeting. Or it could suggest you're too

fussy—not a team player. Either way, it's a bad sublim-
inal message.

Carry a nice pen—you are a writer. The pen is
your most basic tool, your emblem, your icon. Pick
something nice. Not a Montblanc gold-nib fountain
pen—even if you actually have one of those, don't
bring it for taking notes, it's overkill—just use something that says "I am willing to spend $7.98 for a
rollerball pen in a color of my own choosing rather
than make do with the cheesy Vicodin freebie that I
picked up at the reception desk in my psychophar-
macologist's office."

Don't overdress—no suits, male or female. That
shouts "executive." If you're pitching to one, she expects to look better than you. If you're pitching to a
showrunner, you'll make him think of executives and
that is the last person he wants to take ideas from. Stay
away from chic designer ripped jeans or flamboyant
accessories. That's for actors and it focuses way too
much attention on your "look."

Don't underdress—too little attention to your
grooming and it looks like you didn't consider this
meeting important, so no worn-out sneakers, no
frayed polo shirts.

What you want is business casual—clean, relaxed,
and unpretentious.

If you've got a meeting, you will be able to get some scripts and
DVDs of episodes of the show you're meeting about. Ask for them
from the assistant when you're scheduling your appointment.
While you've got that assistant on the phone, be friendly. Not too

friendly, just nice. More than perfunctory, less than unctuous. When you get to your meeting make a point of introducing yourself and thank him for the help he gave you. Keep in mind that the showrunner's assistant is your best friend in the business. He's the one who decides when your script gets put on the desk and if your messages get answered. He will also very likely be asked what he thinks of you and your writing. So be nice.

As you did with preparing to write a spec script, take the time to get familiar with the way the show works and then come up with six to ten ideas.

In the meeting, after you pitch your one- or two-sentence Premise Line, take a breath and see if you can gauge the response level. If they don't say anything, keep going with your story pitch, and keep breathing.

If they say things like "We're already doing something like that," or "Do you have anything else?" that's a pass.

Do not make any attempt to continue pitching an idea that has been passed on. It marks you as inflexible and probably difficult. Do not under any circumstances explain why they haven't heard the best part of the story yet.

Move on to your next idea with enthusiasm. How do you do that when you've just been rejected? I have a tool that I guarantee will work if you use it.

Say Cheese

That's it. That's the tool. You smile.

I learned this from a partner I once worked with. She has a natural smile that rivals Julia Roberts's—and she smiles all the time. I think it's to cover free-floating anxiety, but, whatever the reason, the smile works like magic in meetings. Everybody loves her. She also happens to be a very good writer, which is, of course, the most important key to her success, but you cannot underestimate the likeability factor.

A smile works on two levels:

1. The public face. Reacting with a smile shows that you understand it's not personal, which puts the people you're pitching to at ease. A lot of showrunners are fairly compassionate people. They know how much you want a yes. When you smile after you get a no, they're relieved to see you're not desperate for approval.

2. The inner demon. A smile will actually relax you, too, and turn the disappointment at losing the last pitch into enthusiasm for the next one. That enthusiasm comes across as charisma. So smile. Fake it if necessary—it will still work—and then move on to your next idea.

TOOL BOX

SMILE

Use a smile in the middle of conversations when not much is on the line and observe the effect on both your listener and your own internal state. Does this seem like an idiotic idea? Do you think it will turn you into a bobbleheaded happy face? It might, but experiment with it.

I myself am not a natural smiler; in fact, my default look is kind of a scowl, or at least it used to be, so I devised a training program for myself. Here's what I did:

I started making a conscious effort to smile in low-stakes situations where nobody really cared about me one way or the other, like when I ordered in a restaurant, paid the valet parking guy, or signed my credit card slip at a Target checkout. I noticed how it felt easier to get a conversation going. I'd make a little joke, we'd have a little laugh, life was good.

I raised the risk factor and tried smiling under tense situations where it could benefit me if the other person found me charming: getting seated at a crowded restaurant without a reservation, disputing a car repair bill, stopping someone from cutting in front of me in line. It was foolproof. If I smiled, I felt better, communication was smoother, and I wound up getting pretty much what I wanted about 90 percent of the time.

If you do this on a daily basis, it will become a natural part of you. As you raise the degree of difficulty, you will hit the sweet spot of your "smile naturally" comfort zone—say, somewhere between cajoling the registrar at your child's nursery school and placating the judge in an army court-martial.

Take Yes for an Answer

If the people* you're pitching to are interested in the story, they'll start riffing on the idea. And changing it! That's great! Executive Producers don't change stories they aren't interested

---

*I say people because usually there will be at least three or four staff writers in the meeting. One time I pitched to a room of thirteen writers, and they all felt compelled to speak, do jokes, and generally dominate the pitch session. I didn't sell a story that day, but I heard later that a couple of those writers were dropped. There were just too many writers for the room.

in. If they're riffing and changing stuff, you've captured their imagination, they're thinking about how it fits in with their show. Don't argue or cling to your original idea.

Another crucially important principle that I learned from Mark Ganzel (see Structure Chart, Chapter 10) was the concept of "Yes, and . . ." Before becoming a writer, Mark had been an improv actor and the principle of "Yes, and . . ." is basic to the technique. It's simply that you do not negate what another player has established. You acknowledge it and then you can add to it something of your own.

There is no better guideline for participation on a writing staff or for getting notes from superiors than the principle of "Yes, and . . ." (or just getting along in the world, for that matter). Thinking "Yes, and . . ." creates an attitude of acceptance instead of resistance. You don't even have to add anything, just thinking it is enough.

So if producers are changing your idea, go directly to "Yes, and . . ." mode and start taking notes. You may have just sold a story. "Yes, and . . . I'll get started on the outline right away" is a really good way to end a meeting.

Fear and Trembling

You're going to be nervous. Don't deny your nerves. Accept them. Invite them in; they're coming anyway, you might as well offer them a chair. They just may sit quietly and let you get on with what you're there to do. Actually, if you're new to this game, people expect you to be nervous when you pitch. It can even be kind of charming. It says you think they're important enough to be nervous.

You want to know my personal worst pitching experience? Of course you do.

It was early in my career. I'd written a few episodes for a couple of popular sitcoms, and I was starting to get meetings to pitch my own ideas for pilots.

Great. My agent's happy and I'm excited about the prospect of having something impressive to put in my high school reunion booklet.

So, I'm in this hotshot studio executive's office pitching my show, when he gets up from his sleek glass-top desk and goes into his adjoining private bathroom, where he proceeds to do what most people do in the bathroom, leaving the door open and instructing me to "Keep going, I can hear you."

Nice.

Pitching on Staff

If you reach your goal of being offered a staff job, don't think you are off the pitching hook. As a staff writer you will be sitting at the table in the writers' room every day for many hours a day—depending on your showrunner's home life, it could be 24—and what you will be doing at the writer's table is pitching. You will pitch lines, fixes, jokes, cuts, ideas for other writers' story problems, and most important, you will be expected to pitch story ideas for episodes.

If you're not an active contributor at the table, you don't belong on staff. You must have the confidence to pitch ideas, many of them bad. It's much better to have pitched a bad idea than never to have pitched at all. Bad ideas lead to good ones. Almost all your pitches, good and bad, will be rejected. It's not you, it happens to everybody. You have to be resilient enough and thick-skinned enough to come back with more. Pitching is a primary skill in a television writer's life. If you're not comfortable doing it, get some support and push past your comfort level. Then keep practicing. It's essential.

But let's back up. Before you even get to pitch stories to a showrunner, you are going to have to get your spec script read. And for that you are going to have to maneuver in . . .

20. THE BUSINESS

The Ten Commandments of Show Business:

IT'S WHO YOU KNOW

NOBODY DOES IT ALONE

Notice there are only two; everything is shorter in television. These are the only absolutely true things I know about Hollywood. Anything else anybody says about Hollywood can be argued, disputed, proved, and disproved by anecdotal evidence, but these two commandments truly *are* written in stone.

It's Who You Know

If you want to work in show business, you must get to know people in the business. How do you make friends and expand your circle of contacts? Contacts can be made anywhere—industry functions, seminars, pitch festivals, openings, parties, even your spouse's cousin's baby's baptism. You never know.

But it's not enough just to go; you have to actively put yourself out there. The official showbiz word for this is *schmooze*. In show business, schmoozing is like breathing. But you're a writer and schmoozing may not come naturally to you. You may need some help to pull you away from the chip dip table, or the bar, depending on your defense mechanism of choice.

Help is here.

Working a Room

My colleague Larry Kohn is an expert in the field of client development for lawyers, accountants, and business managers. He created a list for his clients to challenge preconceived notions about meeting business contacts. I think they are great schmoozing tips, and he's given me permission to adapt his list for writers.

Larry Kohn's Counterintuitive Moves for Working a Room as Interpreted by Ellen Sandler*

Don't try to be charming

Conventional wisdom suggests that working a room is a social process where people need to demonstrate their charm. This is a myth. You don't need to entertain or impress people. It's not about you. There, isn't that a relief? Don't you feel better already?

You don't even need to be interesting; what you do need to be is *interested*. Your strategy is to think of schmoozing as *research*— a task with which most writers already feel comfortable. Ask

---

*You can see Larry's original list, along with many other helpful marketing tips, on his website: www.KohnCommunications.com.

questions. Find out what the other guy is into—forget about trying to impress him; he'll be much happier impressing you.

Big gatherings are great, but go to small ones too

You can only have quality conversations with a handful of people. It may seem like the bigger the party the more people you'll meet, but in reality a large crowd can feel overwhelming and make you even shyer. A small group can be more relaxed and make it easier to meet people. Plus, people won't be as distracted, eyeing the crowd over your shoulder, wondering if they should move on and meet somebody else.

Expand your interests

Consider going somewhere that's interesting to the people you want to meet, even if it isn't your first choice for a fun night. Remember, you're working.

Avoid your friends

One of the biggest mistakes people make when working a room is to go with their friends and inevitably stay with them throughout the evening, huddling together for safety. Your goal is to meet new people, so be brave and go alone or, if you do go with a friend, make a conscious effort not to hang out together. Instead, fan out and cover more territory, then introduce each other to whomever you've met.

Don't come fashionably late

It's harder to break into groups already engaged in conversation. If you arrive early, it will be easier to visit with other early arrivals. In fact, it will be rude not to. You will have made a few acquaintances who can then introduce you to some of their friends as more people arrive.

Pick the longest drink or food line

Usually, you want to get a drink as soon as possible; however, a long line gives you the chance to talk with the person in front of you and in back of you. The longer the line, the more time you have to get acquainted. But you'll probably need to make the first move to open a conversation.

Stop talking

Don't go into detail about what you do or what you're working on. You already know about you; spend your time finding out what other people do. Research. You're there to find out who they are. Do reveal some personal things about yourself; it's a conversation, not an interrogation. But be careful, not too much—this is your new friend, not your new therapist.

Don't worry about giving out your card

Get theirs! Old-school sales techniques stress handing out your card, but that doesn't give you control of the follow-up. Of course, you can give them your card, but it's much more important to *always get their card.* If you've got their card, you are in a better position to stay in touch and build a relationship over time. A bonus is that by not giving out your card, you avoid being bothered by people you don't want to hear from in the future.

Get the cards from people you *don't* want to talk to

If you find yourself cornered by someone you'd like to get away from, the best and quickest way to end the conversation is to ask for their card. When you do, you can comfortably excuse yourself and move on. But if you use this trick, make an extra effort to be polite and kind. You never know!

Anybody can turn out to be somebody. I was just starting in the business, and I was working on a project with a busy TV producer. Every time I went to his office, I'd have to wait for about a half hour for my meeting. I might have gotten irritated and given his assistant, Les, a hard time, but he was a cute guy who had been an actor and so we'd always talk and joke about our New York theater days like refugees from the old country.

Years later when CBS developed and shot my pilot, *Cass,* I was glad I hadn't been rude to or ignored that assistant, because by now Les Moonves was president of the network.

Don't leave early

Most people at Hollywood parties like to get to the valet parking guys before the rush. But hang around; you'll have more opportunities to talk with people under calmer circumstances. Often they're the people in charge of the event or officers in the organization and they may turn out to be your best contacts of the night.

Aim low

The typical Hollywood shark thinks he has to pounce on a potential contact immediately. Well, maybe—it's probably worked in some instances—but I think when you meet someone at a party, a conference, any social situation, it's better not to rush the relationship. You don't have to sell yourself or pitch your script on the spot. You'll seem too hungry. Nothing turns people off faster than desperation.

Much better to just get to know the person. If someone asks you what you're working on, give them your one-sentence what-it's-about line and turn the conversation back to something about them. If you create some rapport, you'll be able to arrange to pitch or send them the script at another time. That's better anyway; you want to extend the relationship.

By using these counterintuitive techniques you'll feel in control of what you're doing, which will make you more confident. You won't feel pressured to sell your project on the spot, which will take a lot of pressure off. You'll meet more people, and you'll learn more about them. The information you get will make it easier to connect, easier to follow up, and easier to build a relationship, which is what contacts are all about.

Nobody Does It Alone

But a writer does not live by contacts alone. You must build a community out of those contacts. A group of peers who'll give you moral support when you're struggling, critical support when you need it, and industry buzz to keep you in the loop.

One of the points I want to emphasize in this book is how collaborative TV writing is and how dependent a career is on help from peers and professionals. I'm sure you have noticed how many people I've cited in this book whose work and skills have helped me in my career and in my development as a writer and a professional. I've done nothing alone.

How do you build a community? First, I believe, you contribute, you don't just get. To paraphrase the words of John F. Kennedy, "Ask not what your contacts can do for you, ask what you can do for your contacts." Be generous. Share scripts, sources, books, and by all means, rejoice in others' successes.

Make an effort to support your friends. Call up and

congratulate someone who just got a job. Make a big deal about it and genuinely wish them well. Go to their openings, recognize their awards, go to their celebration parties—give them one if they're a close friend. It will take your mind off how envious you are and you may also get to meet the people they know.

The truth is their success could be the best thing that ever happened to you. You now know somebody who may be in a position to help you get hired somewhere. People like having their friends around, especially if their friends are supportive and laugh at their jokes.

Scriptwriting is not a zero sum game. Your friend's script being accepted doesn't mean she's taken your spot. Yes it's competitive, yes there are only a few jobs, but if you excel, there is room for you too. This industry always needs another great writer with polished skills and a good attitude who's eager to work long hours and turn out pages by the hundreds.

When you do get help of any kind from someone, be sure to express your appreciation. In word and deed if you can. No one ever feels they get enough recognition, and the truth is they probably don't. Any time you can acknowledge someone else, do. How could it not be a good thing?

21. NOW THAT YOU KNOW SOME PEOPLE

What are you going to do with all those cards you've collected?

Cold Calling

Maybe you've met someone who's given you a lead to someone else who might read your script, or maybe you're brave enough to cold call people. When you call them, you'll need to introduce yourself and give them a one-line pitch about your spec. "Hi, I'm Chris Smith, I've been a journalist for five years (or "I just graduated from the UCLA Screenwriters Program," or "I'm a playwright, and I won a DramaLogue Award for my comedy") and I've written a spec *Desperate Housewives* that I'd like to ask you to read." Take a breath, their turn to speak: "Uh huh."

Now, you again. "It's about what happens to Susan's relationship with Lynette and the other neighbors when she reports Tom for child abuse after she witnesses him using corporal punishment on his kids." Them: "Oh, uh huh." You: "It's based on an incident I covered when I was an investigative reporter for the *Sacramento Bee*." (Or as a social worker with the Denver department of child welfare/worked a mothers' support hotline/a babysitter. Whatever it is that gives you a personal claim to the story will pique interest.)

Another breath, time for them to speak: "Oh." You: "May I send it to you? I can email it in a Final Draft attachment or I can send you a hard copy." And that's all you need. I'd be interested in reading something from this writer.

Notice how you want to include something that identifies you as a writer in your introduction. If you feel that you have nothing that identifies you as a legitimate writer, do something about that. Nobody gets drafted out of the stands in Yankee Stadium to play major league baseball; they have to have some kind of playing experience somewhere. Network television is the major leagues, and if you want to write for it, you need to have written something besides a spec script. At the very least, you can take a class or enter a writing contest; then you can say you have studied with this instructor, or won that award. You will be building an identity as a writer.

Are you an authority in another field? That counts! Bring that authority to bear on your writing. I had a client who was an aerospace engineer and wrote a *Commander in Chief* spec based on her actual experience working for NASA. Her professional background definitely impressed people and they wanted to see what she wrote. I know a writer who is also a practicing attorney; her expertise has made her a valued writer on legal shows.

The point is that you want to give people an idea of who you are and why they might be interested in reading your work, how you bring something unique to your writing. Do this briefly. Do NOT recite a list of your credits, they'll be gone before you even mention your script. Choose *one*, your most significant credit, and use that to introduce yourself. Then, if you want to include a résumé with your script submission you can.

Put It in Writing

Often you'll need to contact someone for the first time with a query letter. Keep it simple and don't expect to sell your script in the letter. Think of your letter as a *TV Guide* log line about you. How much do you want to read when you're looking at TV listings? Not that much, right? Do the same thing in the query letter as you would do in the cold call described above. The intent of any query letter is NOT to make a sale but to get permission to send your script.

This recent email exchange is an excellent example of what *not* to do. It's not the worst; in fact, the mistakes are fairly typical, which is why I've deconstructed it to show where the writer went wrong and how you might handle the same thing better.

> From: IM@Outofit.com
> Sent: Wednesday, August 04, 200X 9:00 PM
> To: ellen@SandlerInk.com
> Subject: Sitcom Treatment
>
> Dear Ellen,
> S—— suggested I contact you regarding my sitcom treatment. I have gotten excellent feedback from various people associated with NBC and ABC, but now I want to make sure it is really sharp AND I want to partner with the right people who can get to the right showrunner.
>
> The concept is totally fresh and the content is an advertiser's dream. It has a built-in audience, and it is perfect for cameos. The material is so readily available and endless, a fine writer could take my stories and write a season's worth of shows with little effort.

Intrigued? May I send it to you? How would we proceed? What is your fee?

Woof,
I. M. Outofit

So many errors, and in such a short document! She starts out fine, with a referral, "S—— suggested I contact you..." But then it goes downhill . . . fast:

> I have gotten excellent feedback from various people associated with NBC and ABC, but now I want to make sure it is really sharp AND I want to partner with the right people who can get to the right showrunner.

She made **Mistake #1:** Trying too hard to impress. Compounded by **Mistake #2:** Asking for more than is reasonable.

She tells me how impressed other people are with her project, but she doesn't get across what she wants from me. It seems like she wants me to pick up her idea and package it and sell it for her. A) If that's what she wants, she's too vague, making me guess, and B) If that *is* what she wants, that's a lot to ask a stranger in an email. Maybe her instincts told her it was too much to ask, so she tried to hide it by being fuzzy. It doesn't work.

I'm thinking: "Who are 'the right people'? Do you think I'm 'the right people'? Do you think I know 'the right people'? Do you think I'm going to partner with you and get you to 'the right people'? Why would you think I'd want to do that for you? I don't even know you!" So right away I'm put off, or, if I'm being compassionate and generous, I'm thinking, "Well, she really just doesn't have a clue as to how the business works."

Slow down, take smaller steps. You'll be less likely to trip and fall. If you really have gotten some interest from NBC or ABC, be specific.

Better choice:

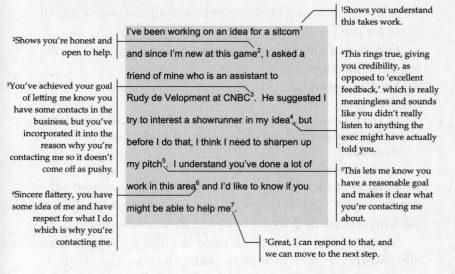

[1]Shows you understand this takes work.

[2]Shows you're honest and open to help.

[3]You've achieved your goal of letting me know you have some contacts in the business, but you've incorporated it into the reason why you're contacting me so it doesn't come off as pushy.

[4]This rings true, giving you credibility, as opposed to 'excellent feedback,' which is really meaningless and sounds like you didn't really listen to anything the exec might have actually told you.

[5]This lets me know you have a reasonable goal and makes it clear what you're contacting me about.

[6]Sincere flattery, you have some idea of me and have respect for what I do which is why you're contacting me.

[7]Great, I can respond to that, and we can move to the next step.

I've been working on an idea for a sitcom[1] and since I'm new at this game[2], I asked a friend of mine who is an assistant to Rudy de Velopment at CNBC[3]. He suggested I try to interest a showrunner in my idea[4], but before I do that, I think I need to sharpen up my pitch[5]. I understand you've done a lot of work in this area[6] and I'd like to know if you might be able to help me[7].

That is all that would be necessary to have an effective communication. But let's examine the rest of what she wrote, because it does get worse.

When she wrote:

> The concept is totally fresh and the content is an advertiser's dream. It has a built-in audience, and it is perfect for cameos.

She made **Mistake #3:** Overselling.

These are value judgments. *Her* value judgments. In fact, her opinions don't matter. These are the things that the buyer should be allowed to decide for himself. The impression I. M. gives here is that she knows the buyer's business better than he does himself, which, though I'm sure she doesn't intend it, comes off as arrogant.

Her effort to sound like a pro who knows her stuff actually has the reverse effect, making her sound like an amateur.

Better choice:
Don't mention any value judgments at all. Let your material speak for itself.

And then, if I might have been inclined to forgive her for being naïve, she delivers . . .

The Unforgivable:

> The material is so readily available and endless, a fine writer could take my stories and write a season's worth of shows with little effort.

Mistake #4: Adding insult to injury. Don't ever use the words "stories" and "little effort" in the same sentence! And to say "fine writer" in this context is just plain condescending.

Expecting someone to want to do the heavy lifting of actually realizing a story in writing while she does the relatively breezy task of coming up with "endless" ideas for stories is downright insulting and shows a complete lack of understanding of how creating a show for television works.

Better choice:
Showing some humility would make your listener more likely to consider helping you. Something like this:

> "I am hoping that you find my material interesting and that you can see a show here."

When she wrote:

> Intrigued?

She made **Mistake #5:** Begging for "no." It's dangerous to ask a question that has only two possible answers, one of them being "no." This marks her, not as intriguing, but rather as presumptuous, because, of course, she is assuming the answer to be "yes," or why would she ask.

Better choice:
Don't ask.

She ends with:

> May I send it to you? How would we proceed? What is your fee?

These questions are not mistakes in themselves, but since she has not really made it clear what she wants from me, they're hard to answer meaningfully. Plus, three questions one right after the other makes me feel assaulted.
Better choice:

> What sort of fee do you charge to look at material?

Then she closes with:

> Woof,

Mistake #6: Too cute/obscure/weird. Whatever does she mean by this? I don't get it, and if she meant it to be funny it misses big-time. (Later, I find out that her idea is about a dog walker, but I had no clue when I first read it.)
Better choice:
A simple "Thank you." Or, "I look forward to hearing from you."
But wait, she's not done:
Four minutes later (check the time stamp!), she sends another email.

From: IM@Outofit.com
Sent: Wednesday, August 04, 200X 9:04 PM
To: ellen@Sandlerink.com
Subject: P.S.

> "Coach" was one of the best-written shows on television! I.M.

Mistake #7: P.S.?! An afterthought? Ineffective sucking-up.
Better choice:
Don't judge a show I worked on, even favorably. Instead be specific, tell me how you relate to my work and I'll really appreciate it.

> "I know you wrote for 'Coach,' which was one of my favorite shows. I especially loved your episode when they went skiing and Coach panicked on the black diamond slope. I did the same thing and even broke my leg just like he did."

Okay, what if you don't remember a specific episode that I wrote, but you want me to know you liked the show a lot? Still be specific about why you liked it.

> "I know you wrote for 'Coach,' a show I especially liked because it was the only one I know of that had a middle-aged man with an age-appropriate wife that he really seemed to like and respect."

This shows me you have actually given your praise some thought, and that's impressive.
So here's my reply:

On Aug 5, 200X, at 12:55 AM, ellen@SandlerInk.com wrote:

Dear I.M.,
    Thanks so much for your interest. My consultation work focuses on three elements of career building: 1) clarification of ideas and content, 2) pitching and presentation skills, and 3) career strategies.
    If you email me a time and a phone number, I'll be happy to call and discuss the possibilities with you. You can check my credentials on my website: www.SandlerInk.com.

    I look forward to talking with you,
    ES

I've given very specific, simple instructions as to how I want to communicate with her.

What I get back from her:

From: IM@Outofit.com
Sent: Thursday, August 05, 200X 5:13 AM
To: ellen@SandlerInk.com
Subject: Re: Sitcom Treatment

> Thank you, Ellen.
> I have already checked out the website.
> I will call today.
>
> I.M.

Mistake #8: Call?! She plans to bypass my procedure.

I'm annoyed. The last thing I want is for her to call me and I'm spending time figuring out how I'm going to communicate with her. Not only is she clueless, but she's also high maintenance.

Better choice:

Follow directions! Send me an email with a phone number and a time to call, like I said. That communicates respect and cooperation and that's what anyone is going to want from you if they're going to consider being in business with you. Wasn't that the reason you wrote to them in the first place?

22. AGENTS AND MANAGERS

What's the Difference?

Agents take 10 percent of your earnings, managers take 15 percent. Agents are licensed, managers are not. Managers may attach themselves to your material in a producing position; agents are prohibited by law from doing that, which is why many agents have left agenting and turned into managers.

Managers I've talked with tell me they are more open to taking on younger, less experienced clients than agents are, and often help their clients get agents. They also take a stronger hand in shaping your career. Managers will give you input on your material, agents usually won't. (My agent has never given me a writing note.) Writing notes from a manager could be more important for a film writer than a TV writer, who will be working on a staff where there will be plenty of input from the showrunner.

Do you need both? I've never had a manager, but the business gets more competitive every day and many people feel it's worthwhile to have more than just one person looking out for you. If you do take on both, you'll want to make sure your agent and your manager respect each other and are comfortable working together. If they're not, you should probably drop one. You don't need that kind of conflict.

Who Gets You Work?

You get yourself work. Your writing, your contacts, and your reputation get you work. Without that, there's very little an agent can do for you, which is why they aren't eager to represent new writers. You do not necessarily need an agent or a manager to get a job and, in fact, you will most likely have to find your first job yourself. Moreover, if you get yourself a job, you will then most certainly find an agent willing to represent you. If you do have a job offer you should definitely have a professional representative negotiate the deal for you, because that's what agents do: protect your interests and get you a better deal.

I was meeting with an Executive Producer of a new show who had just hired me. As we were talking, she said to me with a kind of desperation in her voice, "Do you know any good writers?" I looked around her spacious office; there were, I don't know, hundreds of scripts, covering the floor. Stacks and stacks of them, and every one had an agency cover on it. All those submissions by agents and she's asking *me* for a recommendation!

I told her about a friend whose work I liked, and guess what? She read him and brought him on board.

Once you've got a credit, then an agent has stuff to work with. He can submit you for staffing jobs with a reasonable expectation that you will be read. But again, the quality of your script is what generates further interest, not your agent. The president of William Morris can't get you a job if the response to your writing isn't there.

After You Get One

Things will seem a little easier once you have an agent or a manager. They do know the town; the studios and production companies who wouldn't accept scripts from you will accept them from your agent or manager. But depending solely on your representatives to get you jobs is the road to deep dissatisfaction and bitterness. You'll meet writers who expect their agent to do everything; they are the ones you hear complaining about how bad their agent is or how little their manager does and how they have to get a new one every six months.

> AGENT:
> . . . I'm not your mother. I don't find plays for you to star in. I field offers. That's what I do.
> —FROM *TOOTSIE* BY LARRY GELBART
> AND MURRAY SCHISGAL

It's your career and you must work to keep yourself viable. If you don't get a job, presumably your agent has other clients and he'll still make money. You won't. Write new material, make contacts, generate interest. Work *with* your agent or manager.

For example: You meet another writer, a Supervising Producer of a TV show, you hit it off and he'd like to take a look at your script. You call your agent or manager and ask her to please send your stuff over to the producer you just met. That sets up a comfort zone for everybody. You make the contact, generate the interest, your representative sends your stuff, talks you up, and can follow up to push you, which is a lot better than you having to do it. The system appears to work and you don't get all grumpy and blame your agent for not finding work for you.

Here's what manager Adam Peck,* owner of Synchronicity Management in New York and Los Angeles, has to say about what he expects from the writers he represents:

"It's also important that writers not be reluctant to do all the work it requires to succeed in this business, which, on top of writing well, also requires some real networking skills and a sense of politics, both of which can be difficult for many writers.

"I expect them to work as hard as I do and continuously provide me with as much information, ideas, and suggestions about their work and their career trajectory as they can. I see the relationship as a partnership."

---

*You can read a longer interview with Adam Peck on my website: www.SandlerInk.com.

Another Thing

As you have probably already discovered, you will run into difficulty when submitting any material to a major production company on your own. However, if you haven't got an agent or a manager yet and you want to have some representation, there is another option: an entertainment lawyer. That will cost you some money in legal fees, but it will facilitate your script submission and if there is subsequent interest in your work, the lawyer can negotiate your deal.

If you're ready to spend money on a lawyer, invest some money first in your material. Get some professional guidance—classes at the very least, or a private writing coach.* Don't rush your script into circulation until you've gotten a professional response that confirms your confidence in your material.

And since we're on the subject of paying people to help you, I feel obliged to raise a warning flag. Almost everyone I have ever dealt with in the industry has been legit and fair. (They haven't all been nice, but that's another story altogether.) However, there are some people on the periphery of show business who take advantage of writers who don't know their way around yet. People who may not have much more ability to get in doors than you do may pass themselves off as agents or managers. The thing that should set off alarm bells is if they ask you to pay a fee for them to represent you. No legitimate manager or agent will ask you to do so. Their compensation should be only

---

*I offer classes and private coaching, which you can check out on my website, but I am by no means the only one. There are many qualified consultants to choose from. Check credentials carefully. They should have some substantial professional credits either as a writer, studio executive, or teacher.

their agreed upon percentage of your contracted work. They get paid when you get paid. Period.

Take Charge

So what can you do instead of chasing after agents who aren't interested in representing you yet?

Create buzz

Put the effort into getting your work noticed in another venue. Anyplace you can get your work published, or performed, can be a path into the industry.

The list of playwrights now working as television writers is a long one. You don't need to be produced on Broadway. As you read in the beginning of this book, I did a one-act play in a small venue that got me my first job and my first agent. Plays are a viable avenue into either comedy or drama.

Journalism is another good background. A client of mine had written for a number of magazines and journals when he came to me for consultation on his spec script. His discipline and experience enabled him to learn quickly and within a year he had his first staff job on the cable series *Saved*.

My former partner Cindy Chupack wrote a couple of freelance essays for the now-defunct magazine *New York Woman*. When Producer Wendy Goldman was staffing her series *Room for Two*, those essays caught her eye. She brought Cindy out to intern on the pilot. That's how we met and became writing partners.

Can you write some freelance magazine articles? Even if it's a small magazine, publication is validation. It's a credit, it's experience; you learn to be a better writer when you meet a deadline and someone else's demands. It counts.

Many writers get hired on sitcoms after writing for sketch-comedy troupes, working in improv companies, or writing stand-up material (their own or someone else's). A number of writers on *Raymond* were comics who had performed with Ray. Every sitcom staff has at least one writer who's an ace joke writer; late-night talk and variety shows have many. If that's your gift and you prove it by having comics perform your material (or you perform your material), you'll find a job and an agent, I promise you.

Can you write and shoot a short video and put it on the web? Or write a blog about something you care about? If it's fun or outrageous and gets some buzz, people will be calling you. There are junior development executives whose express job is to look out for the next new thing in small, out-of-the-mainstream venues. When people like that start calling you, agents will want to read your spec script.

Enter writing contests. Most script contests cater to feature films, but there are some contests specifically for television scripts. I think that's a good thing, because with fewer contests it's possible for agents and producers to actually follow them, as opposed to screenplay competitions where there are hundreds. Too many winners can dilute the interest among industry professionals. Appendix II is devoted to the ins and outs of television script contests.

Get in the loop

Get a job that puts you in contact with the industry.

Writer's assistant jobs are the most coveted, because you're right there inside the room with the showrunner and all the other writers every day, and if you've got a good spec you're in scoring position. That's the good news; the bad news is that because those jobs are so desirable, they are almost as hard to get as a writing job itself. If you get to know some assistants socially, you will have an inside track when jobs open up.

Agents and managers also have assistants, and you will get to know the business from the inside out if you're working in any capacity at an agency. If you want to get one of these jobs, your computer and organizational skills will need to be first-rate. Other office experience might be good on your résumé, but not essential. If you're smart, ambitious, and can pass for early twenties, you could still be a viable candidate, if not as an assistant then maybe as a receptionist or a runner. Just get in there. Once inside, you're in a position to meet lots of industry people and you may be able to get one of the junior agents to read your spec.

Register with the human resources departments at every studio. There are also temp agencies that specialize in entertainment industry jobs where you can register for employment. Again, you'll be in a better position if you have office skills, but even if you don't, they will have listings for personal assistants who do things like take pets for shampooing and pick up dry cleaning... and isn't that what you went to college for? But seriously—and you are serious, aren't you?—take any job at all that gets you in proximity to someone in the business. Any job where you can meet agents' assistants who may someday become agents, production assistants who may someday be producers, or actors who may someday have recurring roles on shows you want to submit your scripts to, is a good place to start. (The actor probably won't be able to help you, but he'll invite you to his party, where you might meet a writer who could.)

I know a writer with no agent who had a screenplay picked up by Antonio Banderas. How did she get to him? She tutors his kid. But do I need to tell you that just having access wasn't enough? The screenplay was great and on a topic that interested him. Do I also need to tell you she has an agent now?

And finally, probably the simplest and most immediately effective thing you can do for your career (besides writing, of course) is meet other writers. Where? Well, there's no official hangout, but every Starbucks has a couple of people sitting there with laptops open—in L.A. those are usually writers. There are classes, writer's groups, online chat rooms, writer's pitch fests, and conferences. Some Writers Guild programs are open to nonmembers. You can learn about all of these opportunities in writer's magazines and local L.A. weeklies. Subscribe to them and go to the advertised events. (See Appendix III: Sources.)

Get involved in any way that makes sense for your circumstances. That's your work when you're working on your career. And of course, when you do go somewhere, don't wait for someone to introduce himself or herself to you. These are writers. They are just as introverted and shy as you. Put yourself out there.

> **Advice on** how to break into the business from manager
> Adam Peck:*
>   "There's no recipe, just keep writing and refining your
> work. Get in any way you can and keep learning about the
> business, making contacts, and constantly evaluating what
> makes you happiest and fulfilled as a writer."

Does this sound like a lot of effort? It should, because it is.
But I think it's more likely to get you results than cold calling
agents, begging them to read your stuff, and constantly being
turned away. That can make you depressed and bitter really fast,
and that's not going to be a good place to be coming from. You
can put your effort into getting an agent or you can put your
effort into getting work. I suggest the latter; the former will
follow.

---

*Read more advice from Adam on my website, www.SandlerInk.com.

23. TO LIVE AND DIE IN L.A.

It sounds like you have to be in Los Angeles, doesn't it? Well, if you want to work in TV production, you do. Like any other migrant worker, you've got to go where the work is, and nearly all network television is produced in L.A. Certainly the episodic shows that you want to write for are. A few are done in New York and some are shot outside of L.A., because it's cheaper, but most writing jobs are generated in what everyone calls Hollywood, which is, more often than not, actually Burbank.

So what's it take to live in L.A.? A few thousand a month. And that's just for gas! No, really, that's about what you should budget for unless you have circumstances that provide you with free rent and food.

You must have a car. It doesn't have to be a BMW, but it does have to run. Which means $$. You'll need repairs, maintenance, and insurance (and if you park like I do, a good body shop). There really is no way around a car in L.A. There are buses, but you cannot do what you will need to do on buses in L.A. Taxis will cost you more than a car if you plan to be in town longer than a week.

You can live frugally. You don't have to have a pool or join the most exclusive health club, but you do need to go places, take classes, attend openings, and have lunch with people. If you don't do that, you're wasting the rest of your money being in L.A.

There are many other advantages for an aspiring writer in L.A. The Writers Guild and the Museum of Television and Radio sponsor events where writers discuss their work process and there is time for the audience to ask questions. There are often receptions that follow, with opportunities to meet people. Think about inviting another writer to join you—events like these offer a perfect way to follow up with recent contacts.

The UCLA Extension Program offers a number of classes on writing for television, an ideal place to meet and form relationships with other writers. UCLA also hosts writers and book fairs. These events feature speakers, panel discussions, and a courtyard of booths representing organizations in the area. They are great places to find out about businesses that cater to writers, professional associations, and even other schools' programs.

Television tapings and studio tours give a behind-the-scenes look at the goal. Multi-camera sitcoms shoot in front of a live audience. If you are writing for the half-hour format, take the opportunity to watch the writers, directors, actors, and the long list of other studio staff in action. You will get a firsthand look at why you have to limit your sets and avoid crowd scenes in your script. After the third or fourth hour, you'll also know firsthand why "Moving on!" is such a welcome sound.

Tickets are free. Go to www.tvtickets.com, where you can order them and print them out right from your computer.

Let's hear from a young writer I know who recently left a high-paying job as an engineer designing cellphone components for Motorola to come to Los Angeles and pursue a career writing for television. Here, then, is our correspondent reporting live from Los Angeles:

"Just walking your dog in Los Angeles can be an opportunity. I wear a baseball cap with 'WRITER' stitched across the front, and I get stopped by people asking, 'What do you write?'

"They are usually television writers themselves. Although none of them have been looking to hire (some may have even been hoping I was in a position to hire), they were more than happy to give me real man-on-the-street answers to some questions. I've asked them specifics about the shows where they have worked on staff, what they thought were the best new shows of the season, and if they were working on new spec scripts or any other writing projects. (Note: This may only work if you have a dog as cute as mine.)

"But even better is meeting people who are in my same boat: people struggling to work in the competitive field of television writing (or screenwriting, acting, and stand-up). It's encouraging to be around people who understand why it would take six months to write a half-hour show or why even bother if it can't be sold. And the best, since moving to L.A. I haven't heard once that I'm wasting my college degree (well, at least not from anyone who wasn't here just for vacation)."

24. BUT WHAT IF I DON'T WANT TO DIE IN L.A.?

You don't have to. At least not right away. Learn your craft wherever you are at the moment. Write your spec script before you go.

Just about everywhere has local theater companies, comedy clubs, newspapers—get some experience where you are. There are college film and theater departments all over the country with classes in writing. Take what's offered in your area. And you can enter contests from anywhere.

If there are any local film production companies, volunteer for work, make some contacts. If not, try your local TV station. Don't know anybody there? That's what networking is for. You must know somebody who knows somebody there. Volunteer. It could develop into some real work.

When you have a portfolio of material, some local experience, and maybe some money saved up, you can come to L.A. for a period of time and test the waters.

Or not; if you get involved enough where you are, you may decide you don't want to leave. Either way you'll be following your dream, and if you've learned to write a good spec script in the process, you never know where that could lead you.

25. TECH SUPPORT

I have only one thing to say about computer technology: Buy a software program. Either "Movie Magic Screenwriter" (www.write-bros.com) or "Final Draft" (www.finaldraft.com). They will format for you.

Which one should you pick? That's really up to you. I've used them both. They both conform to the industry standard; Final Draft may be more ubiquitous just because it got there first. Either, used properly, will give you a professionally formatted script and they both have great tech support. They cost a little over two hundred dollars, but it's so worth it for the time and trouble they save you.

Actually, I have a second thing to say: SAVE FIRST! When you open a blank document, assign it a name and save that empty doc. Then, as you type, hit Ctrl+S frequently. I have

---

*I'll admit it, I'm electronically challenged and always take the easy way out with computers—that is, I ask my husband for help. But for those of you who are determined to save money, or who love to procrastinate by tinkering with your computer, I've asked my live-in tech guy (said hus-

learned this the very hardest way, and I am chagrined to admit that it took more than one loss for me to finally get it. Ouch. There is just no reason not to save first and save often.

There, we're done with technology.*

---

band, Peter Basch) to write a more detailed discussion of how you can get the most out of your computer software. You can find his report by going to my website, www.SandlerInk.com, and looking under Tools.

26. HOW MANY PRODUCERS DOES IT TAKE . . . ?

As many as a show can afford, because in television producers are, for the most part, writers.

Definitions of Titles

Credits in television are supremely important. Your last job is what your next salary is negotiated from, and without an on-screen credit you didn't have the job.

Writing credits are determined by the Writers Guild and, in a television series, "written by" is the credit given to the writer or writing team who pitched the original story idea and wrote the first draft.

It is standard procedure for all scripts (with the possible exception of those written by the showrunner) to be rewritten by the show's staff. However, the original writer, who is usually also on the staff, will retain the "written by" credit,* which thus determines script payment and residuals. All writers in episodic television receive the Guild minimum for a script on which they hold the "written by" credit.

The producer credits arise so that agents for experienced writers can negotiate for pay to augment the standard script fees and compensate the staff for the week-to-week rewriting and producing work.

When you are hired to write on a TV show staff, your credit is negotiated at the time your deal is made and it is set in your contract before you ever write a word. There are many different producer titles that are determined by your level of experience. Here is a guide for the perplexed:

Executive producer

The showrunner and usually the head writer.† Often the creator of the show, unless he's gone off to create other shows, in which case an experienced writer will be brought in by the production company to replace him. The showrunner is responsible for every aspect of the show: every word of the script, every actor who is cast, every edit, how the budget is spent, everything. Of course, there is an entire crew to do all these jobs, but the showrunner has the responsibility of overseeing everything. Some showrunners delegate more than others.

---

*Traditionally in series television, the original writer retains credit even though much rewriting has been done by the staff. However, there is a trend for some producers to take more credit than perhaps is ethical. In such cases the writer is entitled to request an arbitration by the Guild to determine proper crediting. Should this happen to you, contact the Writers Guild for information, help, and advice.

†One-hour dramas will sometimes have a nonwriting Executive Producer. For example, Jerry Bruckheimer, of the *CSI* franchise and *Without a Trace,* is a nonwriting Executive Producer. Less common with half-hour comedies.

Compensation ranges from high six figures to the stratosphere, especially if the show goes into syndication.

Sometimes there will be more than one Executive Producer credited. A director can also be an Executive Producer, especially if he directed the pilot. Often the star's manager will take an Executive Producer credit and the star herself can have an Executive Producer credit to ensure some control over the show and a bigger piece of the action if the show goes into syndication. There may even be some staff writers who have been on the show for several seasons credited as Executive Producers. All of these Executive Producers can exercise influence over the production, and if the show should win an Emmy they will each get one with their name on it, but they are not the showrunner.

Co-executive producer

A writer who's had a number of years of experience writing on shows at the producer level or above. The Co-EP's primary responsibility is as a staff writer. She'll write several original episodes per season, for which she will receive "written by" credit, as well as rewrite other writers' scripts for which she'll not be credited. A Co-EP supports the EP. She may be involved in reading spec script submissions, taking story pitches, casting sessions, editing sessions, and of course rewrites, but she will not have authority for final decisions. After several successful seasons a Co-EP's title may be upped to Executive Producer, but the level of responsibility is likely to stay the same.

Consulting producer

A writer with a lot of previous experience usually on at least one hit show. It could be someone who's on an expensive overall deal* and the studio wants to lay some of that big money off on the production budget of a show. Or it may be a writer the Executive Producer trusts and likes having around to bounce things off. He is considered part of the writing staff, but may not be there every day. He may only come in for one or two rewrite nights. He may or may not write episodes.

Supervising producer, producer, co-producer

These are all staff writers with varying degrees of experience. They will all come in every day to write scripts, rewrite at the table, attend run-through with the actors, and do whatever the showrunner needs from them, much the same as the Co-EP.

Compensation for all the producer level writers on a prime-time network show range in the mid-six figures and are negotiated by their agents based on previous credits.

Story editor or sometimes executive story editor

A junior writer. In the old days, there really was somebody who edited the freelance scripts that came in. Today, a show will do at best two freelance scripts a season; all the other scripts are staff-written. So now Story Editor is a title for a less experienced writer. She will need to come up with stories, but the only editing she will be doing is on her own script. A story editor will not go up to the stage should the show win an Emmy for Best Comedy or Drama. She will not even get tickets to attend the event, a privilege reserved for producer level or above only. Salary is in the low six figures.

Uncredited staff writer

This is the one title that describes exactly what the person's job is: a writer on the staff who shows up every day, who doesn't go home until he's dismissed, and who receives no on-air credit. If you write a great spec script, take a good meeting, and the

---

*See Showbiz Meanings for Regular Words: A Selective Glossary.

stars align just when you need them, this is likely to be your first job.

You'll receive a "written by" credit for any script that you write, the second draft of which will be entirely changed by all of the writer-producers listed above. Yes, you will get paid a salary on a weekly basis, but it's figured against your script fee when you write your first episode. In other words, you don't get paid an additional script fee in the way the producer-level writers do. Sometimes even your second episode is credited against your salary. It depends on how new you are and what your agent was able to negotiate when he made the deal.

This is a testing period to see if a first-time writer is going to work out. About halfway through the season your option will come up for renewal, and if you're picked up, you'll be upped to story editor and then be credited onscreen. That's when everyone you ever knew, along with some people you never met, will contact you and ask you to get them into show business. You can tell them to buy this book!

There is a producer who does the paperwork, gets the releases, hires crew, and is responsible for the organizational work that makes it possible to shoot the show. In other words, a producer who is not a writer. She is called a line producer. The onscreen credit for this person is signified with a "produced by" credit. The "by" is key. Watch for it on the credits crawl; you'll be one of the few who know the difference.

So now you know the answer to the question that everybody asks as the credits speed by: "Why does a TV show need so many producers?"

27. TO SERVE AND PROTECT

How to police your work. You must copyright any script you write and there are two ways you can do that. You can send it in to the Library of Congress (proper procedures are available on the Web at www.copyright.gov) or you can register your script with the Writers Guild of America. It can be done online at www.wga.org and you do not have to be a member of the WGA to have full benefit and protection. I think this is by far the easier way to go with a television script and it costs a little less as well.

Sue Me

Does a copyright really protect you? Well, it does protect the exact words you wrote down, but you cannot protect or copyright an idea—even an idea for a character or a plot.

Suing a studio or a producer for stealing your idea is a huge expense and "winning" is highly unlikely. Plagiarism is one of the hardest things to prove in court, as a good entertainment lawyer is likely to tell you. Besides, even if you "win" what have you won? If you do get a settlement, you'll wind up paying out most of it in legal fees and you will have seriously diminished your ability to work in Hollywood. Is that really what you want?

I personally know three working writers who did attempt to sue, and let me say that there is a connection between *sue* and *suicide*. None of them got anywhere with their case, and only one of them ever got hired to write professionally again.

You Are Your Own Best Protection

Will people take your ideas? Yes, they might. It's happened to every writer more than once, and no, it's not a happy thing, but you are not just your ideas. As a writer you are the *execution* of your ideas, and that is the most effective protection that you can have.

Ideas are not worth much just as ideas. Everyone has an idea, in fact they have dozens of them, but almost no one can turn those ideas into a good story and get it down on paper in a way that communicates through dramatic action, emotions, and humor. Your craft. Your voice. That is your ultimate protection. People who pay money to people to write aren't looking to steal your ideas; they're willing to pay for you to write them down because they can't and you can. That is the best insurance policy you can have.

What about other writers? They can write it down. Yes, but they will write the same idea in an entirely different way than you do. Your script will survive on its own merit.

I'm not saying ideas won't be stolen from you, I'm just saying don't get hung up on it. Focus on your craft. You'll be fine.

28. AND ANOTHER THING

Rules You Can't Break Under Any Circumstances

- Any script, treatment, proposal, or even email that you send out MUST be clean, correct, and to industry standard. Grammar,* punctuation, spelling, and format must be perfect. No excuses.

- Polite behavior—and that's to everyone: parking attendants, receptionists, waiters, executive assistants. Everyone. No exceptions. You never know who's watching, or listening to you in the elevator. You never know who you'll meet again, or who is friends with the person you met with, and besides, it's just good karma.

- Writers Guild of America rules—even if you're not a member yet, follow the rules. The WGA is the only thing that stands between you and complete exploitation. It's the only reason a writer will ever collect residuals, have

---

*One exception: dialogue does not have to be grammatically correct.

health insurance, or even get a credit on his work in Hollywood. Respect the Guild.

Rules You Don't Have to Follow but You Better Have a Good Excuse Not To

- Laugh at the Jokes—everyone's. Goes for drama too. It brands you as a team player. Very important.

- Meet Your Deadlines—more important than you can imagine in television. A late script causes a domino effect and always costs money. Studios hate that. They don't want it good; they want it now. If you can make it both good *and* now, you'll get known as a genius, and you probably are.

- Respect the People Who Sign the Checks—don't badmouth the company or its projects.

- Don't steal the office supplies.

- Do write a thank-you note for the impersonal corporate Christmas gift. It will be noticed.

- Don't wish bad things on the competition—I tried it, it doesn't help.

- Don't do everything your way—the fastest way I know to be fired.

Now What?

You've got a first-rate spec script. It took you nearly six months to write it, maybe more, but now you've got it. You invested time and effort and cash if you worked with a script consultant or took a class. You've gotten support and encouragement from your family and friends, the feedback from your teachers and other writers tells you that your story flows; the dialogue is fresh yet sounds just like the characters; it's funny, it's touching, it's believable; besides all that, it's the right number of pages . . . and wonder of wonders, an agent *likes* it! Now what?

What Else Ya Got?

People in Hollywood like to avoid burning future bridges, so they will sometimes say they love your script as a way of blowing you off without hurting your feelings. You will know if an agent really does like your work if, after you hear "I love it," you also hear, "What else ya got?"

And you better have something in the works.

Any agent knows that when he sends a writer's material to a producer, if that producer likes what he reads, the first thing he's going to ask is: "What else does she have?"

Why isn't one great script, that you put your heart and soul and six months of your life into, enough? Because, in television, an agent or a producer is not looking at your spec to find a script but to find a *writer.*

Agents have to be able to provide what producers are looking for, and TV producers are looking for writers who write all the time and have lots of stories to tell. If you've got more than one piece of material to show, you demonstrate that you're serious about writing, that you can do the job of a professional writer.

An agent can't sell an episode script, because no one buys an episode script; they hire writers. Series television is primarily staff-written; agents are looking to represent writers who can get placed on staff.

Your spec script is an audition piece. When an actor auditions, if they're really interested, they don't cast him right away, they give him a callback. They want to see him do it again. They want to know he can. It's the same for a writer.

> A professional is someone who can do it again.
> —LIONEL HAMPTON, JAZZ GREAT

People who can hire you want to know that you have range and can write more than one thing. They want to know that you have stamina and can churn out both quality and quantity, because that's what you'll need to do if you're going to be writing television.

So what should your next script be? I have the answer to that. An original pilot. It's a whole different thing and it requires a great deal more heavy lifting. That's gonna take a whole other book. But the good news is, there's no better preparation for pilot writing than learning how to write a great spec script.

Do you feel like an avalanche just fell on you? Not only do you have to write a great script—you have to write more than one, maybe even a bunch. Well, you don't *have* to; you can say this is not for me. But if you want to be a writer in Hollywood you're going to have to write a lot.

Be brave enough to write badly. Be disciplined enough to go back and write better. Repeat as often as necessary until it's good. And then, you know what? Someone will pay you to write even more!

29. LAST WORDS

If you've used the exercises in this book to create your material, you will have learned a process that you can use and adapt for writing any script, including feature-length ones (I even used the process for writing this book). You will have learned it by doing, and therefore it will be a part of you. You will have developed writer's instincts.

Contradictions

I started this book saying that my goal was to tell you the truth. I think I've done that, but just because something is true doesn't mean the opposite is false. It's show business; contradictions abound and one doesn't cancel out the other. What works for one writer may completely stymie another.

Read other books, talk to other writers. You can take almost everything I've said in this book and find someone else who will tell you the opposite. Both positions will probably be right. One thing is true in some cases, the other true under other circumstances.

There is value in the contradictions. Other points of view can shed light on your own already formed opinion. A contradiction may crystallize it or change it, subtly or radically. Embrace the contradictions; turn them over in your mind and see how they might broaden your borders. No one is right all the time about everything, and almost everyone has something to offer once in a while. Be open. Say, "Yes, and . . ." But mainly do the work and figure out what's true for you.

Don't Believe Any Overnight Success Story

It never happens. And if by some miracle it does, you'll know what to do: Call your lawyer.

In the meantime, build yourself a support system to keep your determination from flagging. Set short-term goals and work consistently at them. Take encouragement from small achievements; they will give you the momentum to keep going. Work hard, believe in your project, and then don't look too closely at reality: it can only be discouraging when you're following your dream.

> If I had faced facts, I'd still be in Quincy, Massachusetts.
> —RUTH GORDON, (1915–1988) OSCAR-WINNING
> ACTRESS (ROSEMARY'S BABY, HAROLD AND MAUDE)
> AND SCREENWRITER WITH A SEVEN-DECADE CAREER

Showbiz Meanings For Regular Words
A Selective Glossary

Back End—Money promised to you at a later point, as opposed to "up front" money which you receive immediately upon signing your contract. Back end money generally applies to original material that you create, such as a pilot. You see it only after your show goes into syndication and/or travel cups and T-shirts are sold with your show's logo on them. The percentage is negotiated by your agent and lawyer. It's written into your deal at the time you sell your idea. It can be a great bonanza or a huge legal boondoggle, depending on how the studio wants to interpret your contract after your show has made them a ton of money that they are now sorry they ever agreed to share with you.

Blow—A joke that ends a scene. Etymology on this one is obscure, but some say it came from the '80s, when cocaine use was common.

Button—Same as blow, a scene ender. Still in use, but blow is more current.

Clam—An old joke. A reference that has been so overused it is now a "clam." Viagra is a clam. Publishers Clearing House is an old clam—it was a clam before "clam" was a term. It's considered pathetically lame to use a clam. Pitching such a joke at the table will almost certainly result in awkward silence or cruel mockery. The term is said to have come from the writing room at *Roseanne*. There was an episode about eating clams, and they made so many jokes about actual clams on that episode that it became the generic term for overuse, or so the story goes.

Edgy—Material that pushes at the edge of what is traditional. The tone is often hostile in edgy material. Edgy shows are frequently industry favorites, they get a lot of buzz, and often Emmy nominations, but they usually go unloved by the public and are therefore subject to cancellation. *Arrested Development* was an edgy show that slowly strangled to death. On the other hand, *South Park* is sharply edgy and that has lived to be a legend. But it's also on a cable channel that allows for a broader definition of hit.

Love—A much overused word in Hollywood and it can mean anything from *I really really like you/your script* to *I absolutely hate you/your script*. What it usually means when someone in Hollywood "loves" your spec script is that he is reserving judgment until he finds out if someone more powerful loves it.

New—The holy grail in television. As long as it's pretty much the same as the old stuff.

The Numbers—Not the same as the rackets but possibly as big a gamble. In television, The Numbers are the ratings. The ratings numbers translate into, well, numbers—dollar numbers.

Without sufficient numbers you are off the air; doesn't matter who you are or how much everyone *loves* the show.

Overalls—In showbiz, overalls refer not to work pants but to deals made by a studio with highly successful writer/producers to create new series ideas which the studio hopes to sell to a network. For laying out many millions of dollars, the studio has exclusive rights to anything a writer on an overall comes up with during the period of time of the contract. The studio is gambling that, because the writer has created, or in many cases simply worked on, a monster hit in the past, he will come up with another one, or two, or three. This kind of deal is given out with less frequency now than in the past, though it still exists for the very biggest writers.

Page One Rewrite—Just what it sounds like. Open the script to page one and start rewriting—every word.

Pass—No. In show business "no" is a four-letter word; even the most ruthless agents and the toughest executives do not say the word "no" out loud in public. They say, "We're passing." And it's almost always "we" who pass; no one passes on his own. That way no one can be held responsible when what he passed on turns out to be *The Sopranos.*

Pilot—The first episode of a new show. A pilot episode establishes the characters and their relationships and sets the template for episodes to come. The hope is always that there will be at least one hundred to come. One hundred is the magic number that makes syndication possible, and syndication is the pot of gold at the end of the rainbow; even better than an Emmy—though an Emmy is very, very nice.

Punch Up—Adding jokes to a script, or improving the jokes that are already there.

The Room—Where the writers go every day to work on the scripts. Fourteen hours a day there is not uncommon. It's an inner sanctum and very rarely intruded on by anyone outside of the writing staff and their assistants. Actors, spouses, and network executives are not invited into The Room. Pizza delivery guys, however, are always welcome.

Swing Set—A new set used for one episode. A sitcom is shot on a large studio stage. The regular sets are kept standing throughout the shooting season. There is usually room on the stage for one or two additional sets per episode and it can be pretty much anything—a diner, or a park playground, a store, a doctor's office. Whatever it is, it's called the swing set to distinguish it from the regular sets.

Single-camera shows, especially one-hours, will have regular sets on a sound stage and may also go out on locations for exteriors. Multi-camera shows almost never go to a location. Nearly everything is shot on the stage.

> **On *The Mommies*,** we once had a scene in the backyard of one of the houses and it had a kid's swing set in it. So that week our swing set was actually a swing set.

The Table—What the writers sit around in The Room. Long and utilitarian. Usually covered with pads, pencils, script pages,

M&M's, Red Vines,* and, on comedy shows, silly toys. The showrunner is at the head.† Somewhere near The Table is a writer's assistant putting everything that's said into a computer. At least everything the showrunner says.

Widows & Orphans—A widow is a single line at the bottom of a page—for example, a character name at the bottom of the page with the speech following on the next page. You want to get rid of the single line at the bottom of the page.

Orphan refers to a mostly empty page with only a line or two on it at the end of a scene. (I've heard people use these terms interchangeably.) Fix this by looking for a cut, which will eliminate your extra page, or by adding lines of white space at the bottom of the previous couple of pages so there will be at least $1/4$ of a page on the last page.

---

*Red Vines seem to be to television writers what doughnuts are to cops. I've never worked on a TV show where there wasn't a constant supply.
†On *Raymond*, Phil Rosenthal always sat in the middle of one of the long sides, but it was still the head of the table, because wherever the showrunner sits is the focal point.

Appendix I
The Evolution of a Sitcom Script

People often ask me what a typical production week on a sitcom is like. Here's an article written by Marsha Scarbrough, for *Written By,* the WGA magazine, about my *Everybody Loves Raymond* episode, "No Fat," in which she chronicles the process.

15 Steps to "No Fat"
Written By Marsha Scarbrough

EVERYBODY LOVES RAYMOND
"No Fat"
Written by Ellen Sandler & Susan Van Allen

Step One:
At the beginning of the *Everybody Loves Raymond* season, Ellen Sandler pitches the idea of Marie (Raymond's mother) going on a diet. Since Marie relates to her family through food, changing her relationship to food would create conflict in the family.

Step Two:

Phil Rosenthal responds to the idea of food as a big issue but doesn't want Marie on a diet to lose weight. He suggests Marie and Frank (Raymond's father) change their diets because of high cholesterol.

Step Three:

When the idea is pitched to The Room, Steve Skrovan tells a story about his family suffering through a healthy Thanksgiving dinner. The idea starts to become a story about the family's Thanksgiving being threatened. The stakes are raised by making Thanksgiving Raymond's favorite holiday since he loves his mother's cooking.

Step Four:

An early beat sheet describes all the elements that ultimately end up in the final script . . . and some that don't.

Step Five:

The "two-pager" defines the spine of the story in a condensed narrative. It's rewritten once with Rosenthal's input before being distributed to all the writers and discussed in The Room. The bare bones are: When Marie and Frank learn that they have high cholesterol, Marie goes on a diet for health reasons. Debra (Raymond's wife) coaches Marie in low-fat cooking. Raymond is bereft when he discovers that they are planning to make a tofu turkey for Thanksgiving. Debra insists that they stop thinking of themselves and support Marie. The family gathers for Thanksgiving. While they are politely trying to enjoy the unpalatable dinner, a traditional Thanksgiving feast is delivered from a restaurant. Marie accuses Frank, but Raymond turns out to be the culprit.

Debra is appalled and whisks the food off to their house as the family finishes Marie's dinner.

That night, Raymond hears strange noises in the kitchen and finds Marie with a turkey drumstick. Eventually the whole family ends up chowing down at a midnight feast in the kitchen. In the tag, Marie is in the doctor's office confessing that she couldn't stay on the diet. The doctor suggests eliminating stress from her life. She interprets that to mean that she must control Frank.

After this "two-pager" is refined, it is sent to the network, the studio, and Romano. At this point, Rosenthal suggests that Sandler work with Susan Van Allen on the first draft of the script.

Step Six:

Sandler and Van Allen collaborate by writing some scenes together line by line at the computer and some scenes individually, then trading and revising each other. After a first pass, they solicit input privately from some of the other staff writers and then do a rewrite. That version goes to Rosenthal, who writes notes and jokes in the margins and returns it to Sandler and Van Allen. He questions the need for a scene in the bedroom with Raymond and Debra before they hear the noise in the kitchen. Sandler and Van Allen rewrite, incorporating Rosenthal's notes to create the "writer's first draft."

Step Seven:

The "writer's first draft" goes to the table in The Room. After an hour or more of general discussion on the overall script, the staff starts with the teaser and goes through the script line by line. A writer's assistant types this version into a communal computer as it is being revised. This process may take the better part of two or three days in The Room, but the result is a funnier, faster, more focused script. In this version, Marie blames herself for disappointing her family by not cooking her traditional Thanksgiving dinner, which prompts Ray to voice his support for her need to take care of herself. Also introduced at this point is the idea of Marie and Frank learning about their high cholesterol at a Senior Health Fair. The scenes in the doctor's office are eliminated and the tag is set in a pharmacy where a Senior Health Fair is in progress. A shortened version of the bedroom scene with Raymond and Debra is still in the script.

Step Eight:

The script is sent to Romano, who can only be in The Room when he's not involved in rehearsals on stage. After reading this "table draft," Romano spends a lunch hour in The Room giving his notes on the script page by page. In this case, the changes are minor. He adds a joke and cuts another. A reference to diabetes is changed to "high blood sugar" since, according to Rosenthal, actual diseases aren't funny. Now the script has been "Rayified" and it's ready to go to the stage.

Step Nine:

On a Wednesday morning, cast, director, writers, producers, network executives, studio representatives, and selected crew members meet on the *Raymond* set on Stage 5 at the Warner Brothers lot. After a production meeting, the actors sit around a table and read the script like a play. It gets big laughs. At this point, Romano seems to know the script almost by heart. After the reading, network and studio people huddle briefly with Rosenthal and the writing staff to give notes. The cast begins rehearsals on the stage while the writers return to The Room and make minor revisions. Because there is not enough space on the stage for both the pharmacy set and the bedroom set, the bedroom scene is eliminated. Now Raymond hears suspicious noises in the kitchen from the living room stairs. In response to a network vote to "up the stakes," Marie's cholesterol level is now described as "close to the danger zone."

Step Ten:

On Thursday morning, a new script awaits the cast on stage. They rehearse until 3 P.M., when Rosenthal and the writing staff (who have been working in The Room all morning) come down to the stage for a "Producer's Run-through." They watch the cast perform the script "on its feet" in the sets. After the run-through, Rosenthal freely offers acting and blocking suggestions to the actors and director. The cast is dismissed as Rosenthal and the writers go back to The Room to make revisions based on what they've seen. In this case, a couple of scenes are shortened and a few jokes are honed.

Step Eleven:

On Friday morning, another new script is waiting for the cast when they arrive. Again they rehearse until mid-afternoon, when network executives join Rosenthal and the writers for a "Network Run-through." After watching the cast perform the script with key props, the network execs offer notes and compliments to Rosenthal and the writers. In this case, they express some concerns about the look of the tofu turkey. As Rosenthal works with the actors to fine-tune performances, the theme of the show becomes more clearly defined. Marie's line "I forgot what was important...cooking for my family" in her scene with Raymond becomes the key emotional moment. Rosenthal also shares camera blocking concerns with the director, primarily about the need to show Patricia Heaton (who plays Debra) only from the shoulders up to conceal her very obvious pregnancy. Again the cast is dismissed while Rosenthal and the writers return to The Room and make minor revisions.

Step Twelve:

On Monday morning, the new version of the script goes to the actors and the entire technical crew. The whole day is spent camera blocking with the cast, crew, and director. Rosenthal and the writers stay in The Room and watch the camera setups on a monitor as they work on upcoming scripts. Rosenthal phones his camera notes down to the stage.

Step Thirteen:

Tuesday is Show Day! Rosenthal and the writers work in The Room in the morning while the cast rehearses with cameras on stage. At 12:30, they go to the stage to watch the final run-through. Producers, writers, cast, and crew share a catered meal at 3:30 P.M., then at 5 P.M. the audience comes in and the show begins. During filming, the writers are "on the floor" with Rosenthal and the director. They offer notes and suggestions concerning performances to Rosenthal, who shares them with the actors and director as he feels appropriate. Sandler serves as a liaison between Rosenthal and the "switcher," who is cutting the show live for the audience to see on monitors. It's a critical job, because the switcher's shot choices have a major impact on the laugh track. Tom Caltabiano goes up in the bleachers and interacts with the audience. He fields questions and jokes that it takes 11 writers to write 22 minutes. He also huddles with Romano concerning "take twos," alternate jokes that Romano uses on some second takes to surprise the audience in order to get an equal, if not greater, laugh. Although the "take twos" are written in advance, they are selected by Rosenthal and Romano during filming. To the audience, they appear to be ad-libs.

Craft Service puts out a buffet for the cast and crew. At 8 P.M., the audience is served pizza and sodas to keep them in a jovial mood. After the dinner scene is shot, the tofu turkey is added to the buffet for anyone brave enough to try it. The show wraps and everyone goes home about 11 P.M. Rosenthal proclaims it an excellent filming and says he couldn't be happier. Sandler comments, "More than my initial vision was realized, the core of my original thought is absolutely there and so much better than I ever imagined."

Step Fourteen:

The editor assembles the show based on notes dictated by Rosenthal during filming. Rosenthal finds time to sit with the editor and hone the final cut to perfection. In this case, the tag scene at the Senior Health Fair ends up on the cutting-room floor due to time considerations.

Step Fifteen:

"No Fat" airs during Thanksgiving week.*

---

*Reprinted from May 1999 issue of *Written By,* the magazine of the Writers Guild of America.

Appendix II
Spec Script Competitions

There are contests, workshops, and fellowships that will read new writers' scripts, and many of them are genuinely looking to promote promising new talents. There's a list of reputable contests at the end of this discussion, with websites where you can check the latest deadlines and rules. New contests are always showing up on the horizon, and some screenwriting competitions are expanding to include television spec scripts. Research both on the web and through word of mouth from other writers. The following websites have links to help you keep track of current contests:

www.hollywooditsales.com
www.screenwritersutopia.com

Contests

Many of my students and clients have entered these competitions and, yes, some have even won!* Very exciting.

The insights and suggestions that follow are based on their feedback.

Most contest websites will post a list of past winners and their scripts where you can check out what shows won past awards. If a contest has never honored a cartoon or a cable show, and that's what you want to enter, you may want to inquire if they accept your genre or look elsewhere.

Some contests will have testimonials describing the winners' experiences and successes—what winners are saying about the competitions and what they are doing after winning. You can also find out what other websites or publications are saying about a particular contest.

An established contest will have more industry recognition than a newer or smaller one, so take that into account when deciding which to enter.

Contest prizes can be cash, screenwriting software, a place in a writing workshop, or a read from an industry professional; however, the real prize from a contest win is the visibility and a credential you gain for yourself as a writer. You don't have to win first place to gain from a contest. These competitions have hundreds of submissions, and second, third, finalist, and semifinalist are all accomplishments that will be worthy of note on your résumé.

Some contests will give you feedback on your script. Notes from judges can be very helpful, but there is a skill in interpret-

---

*A recent student of mine won the Austin Film Festival & Competition with her *Scrubs* spec script and went on to get a Disney fellowship. She's now in position to get her first staff-writing job next season.

ing those notes. Not all judges are writers; some may be agents or executives. Their assistants may even be writing the critiques for them, so like all comments from people who do not sign your paycheck, look for consensus as to where problems exist rather than for solutions. It is your job to diagnose why people are having trouble with that scene, and now that you have the tools, you can come up with your own, much better, way to fix it.

As great an accomplishment as it is to win, even winning first place does not mean an automatic job offer, but it will give you some visibility in the industry and some important people will look at your script.

I've spoken to winners who are disappointed by lack of results. My congratulations have sometimes been met with, "Yeah, but it didn't really do anything for me." Well, that's exactly right. Winning doesn't do anything for you unless you do something with your win.

First, of course, put it on your résumé and in your Holiday Letter. Next, use that affirmation as a reason to convince someone to read your work. Now you can contact an agent or a showrunner and tell them you've just won the Such-and-Such Contest and you will up your chances of getting them to take a look at your script.

Finding out what past winners have achieved may help guide you to which agents or other professionals are impressed by certain contest wins. The director of one contest takes an active role in promoting their winners. Each year he asks the winners for a list of people to contact about reading their scripts. Some people just rattle off a list of their favorite television shows and rely on the contest director to convince those shows' producers to give them a read. But the winners who do some of their own research, and perhaps even get personal referrals, are the ones that get read.

Diversity and Minority Fellowship

Several studios have fellowship programs to find and develop diverse* or minority writers. Their goal is to develop new writing talent for the shows they produce.

I've had a number of clients who have been worried about getting into diversity programs for fear of being stereotyped, or because they've heard that the diversity writer isn't taken seriously. That may be true, but I say do it anyway. Any crack in the system is worth exploiting when you're on the outside looking in. The competition is so staggering that anywhere you can get an edge you should grab it. Sometimes the only new writer on a staff is the diversity program writer. If you fit that description, why shouldn't you take advantage of it? These positions are highly sought after and the programs can get thousands of applicants each year. Your minority status isn't a factor beyond the initial point. Once again, your best advantage will be your writing.

No one wants to be thought of only as a "minority writer," but make your stand later when you have options. Turn down any job you want to if you think you're getting locked in and you want to branch out, but not now when you need the help.

I've been hired because I was a female, and I've also been told, "We already have too many women on the staff; we need a gay guy." Grounds for a discrimination suit? Probably, but really not worth the time and money. The show will be off the schedule and the producers will be out of the business before you ever get to court.

Sometimes who you are works for you, sometimes it works against you. You can't change who you are (I hope you wouldn't

---

*Diversity and minorities in television writing may not be the same as in other fields. For example, women are a minority in television writing; so are people over 40.

want to even if you could), so exploit it when it works for you
and move on when it doesn't.

Studio Workshops

Warner Bros. has a unique competition that offers winners a
place in their Writer's Workshop. Unlike the fellowships, this is
not a full-time position and there is a fee to participate. The
workshop involves a weekly educational class with outside
writing assignments.

Getting into this program is a terrific opportunity, because
they are looking to develop new writing talent that they can
place in staff writing positions. But being accepted into the
workshop is no guarantee they will be able to, or even want to,
place you on a show. The efforts you make—your attitude, your
growth and development—while in the program are what will
get you to the next level.

If you are selected to participate, know that it will demand a
major time commitment. If you are like most of the chosen writers, you will probably be working at another job. If you can
possibly take time off while in this program, it would be a
worthwhile investment. I've heard several participants say they
wish they had devoted more time to the program, and I've never
heard anyone say they put too much time into it.

You Win Some, You Lose Some

It's very common for the same scripts to be entered into a variety of contests. A script that wins one contest may not even be a

finalist in another contest. Don't bother to second-guess a contest. No one can write a script that is going to be universally liked, and trying to please everyone is just going to kill your unique voice.

> I don't know the key to success, but the key to failure is trying to please everybody.
>
> —BILL COSBY

Is it worthwhile to enter more than one writing sample in the same competition? (First check if they will allow multiple entries. The ones that require an entrance fee generally will.) Looking at contest results, you may discover the same writer's name more than once. If you think you can benefit from more than one entry, then why not? On the other hand, don't send in a bunch of scripts just to give yourself more chances. If your script isn't really ready, your strategy will likely backfire. You're much better off with one great script than three okay scripts.

There can be a long lag time between the time you turn in your entry and the time you find out the results. Don't sit around waiting—don't ever sit around waiting. Get to work on your next script. You'll need it no matter what happens. If you win, people will want to see more of your work. If you are already at work on your next script and you don't win, it will make the loss a lot easier to take. Starting a new project after a disappointing rejection is tough. If you are already into it, you won't have such a struggle.

Winning these competitions can build your confidence, but

if you don't come out on top, you can use the experience as a test of how well you handle rejection. Rejection and disappointment are part of anyone's career in television. Most things don't work out in any business; in show business the ratio of success to failure is even greater. The biggest difference between the people who succeed and those who don't is not in how much or how often they win, it's how fast they get back up after they lose.

Contests:

Acclaim TV Script Competition:
www.acclaimtv.netfirms.com

American Accolades:
www.americanaccolades.com

Austin Film Festival & Competition:
www.austinfilmfestival.com

Carl Sautter Memorial Television Outreach Program:
www.scriptwritersnetwork.org/tvrech.asp

The Other Network TV Writing Contest:
www.uncabaret.com

Scriptapalooza:
www.scriptapaloozatv.com

Spec Scriptacular Competition:
www.tvwriter.com

TalentScout Management TV Writing Contest:
www.atalentscout.com

Studio workshops:

Warner Bros. Television Writers Workshop:
www.warnerbros.com/writersworkshop

Diversity and fellowship programs:

ABC Entertainment and The Walt Disney Studios Writing
Fellowship Program:
www.abctalentdevelopment.com

CBS Diversity Institute Writers Mentoring Program:
www.cbsdiversity.com

Diverse City NBC Writers on the Verse:
www.diversitynbc.com

Fox Diversity:
www.fox.com/diversity/programs.htm. They will only look
at original pilots.

Nick Writing Fellowship:
www.nickwriting.com

WGA Writer's Training Program:
www.wga.org/subpage_writingtools.aspx?id=933 or
www.wgaeast.org/wtp/

You register with the WGA as a potential participant, then
it's up to you to contact the showrunners and convince them to
hire you. This program is not likely to open up a door initially,
but if you've gotten your script to a showrunner and he likes
what you've written, this works as a low-risk incentive to give
you a trial, because the WGA allows them to pay an official
trainee less than a staff writer.

Appendix III
Sources

Entertainment Bookstores

Samuel French Bookstores
7623 Sunset Blvd.
Hollywood, CA 90046
(323) 876–0570

45 West 25th Street
New York, NY 10010
(212) 206–8990

11963 Ventura Blvd.
Studio City, CA 91604
(818) 762–0535
samuelfrench.com/store

100 Lombard Street
Toronto, Ont., Canada M5C 1M3
(416) 363–3536

Larry Edmunds Bookshop, Inc.
6644 Hollywood Blvd.
Los Angeles, CA 90028
(323) 463-3273
www.larryedmunds.com

Book Castle's Movie World
212 N. San Fernando Blvd.
Burbank, CA 91502
(818) 845-1563
www.bookcastlesmovieworld.com

Book City Script Shop
8913 Lankershim Blvd.
Sun Valley, CA 91352
(818) 767-5194
www.bookcity.net

Book Soup
8818 Sunset Blvd.
West Hollywood, CA 90069
(310) 659-3110 or 1-800-764-BOOK
www.booksoup.com

Drama Book Shop
250 W. 40th Street
New York, NY 10018
(212) 944-0595
www.dramabookshop.com

The Writers Store
2040 Westwood Blvd.
Los Angeles, CA 90025
(866) 229–7483
www.writersstore.com

Libraries

Writers Guild Foundation Shavelson-Webb Library
7000 W. Third Street
Los Angeles, CA 90048
(323) 782–4544
www.wgfoundation.org/library.htm

Margaret Herrick Library (Academy of Motion Pictures Library)
333 S. La Cienega Blvd.
Beverly Hills, CA 90211
(310) 247–3000
www.oscars.org/mhl/index.html

Louis B. Mayer Library American Film Institute
2021 N. Western Avenue
Los Angeles, CA 90027
(323) 856–7654
www.afi.com/about/library.aspx

UCLA Young Research Library Special Arts Library
(310) 825–7253 (must call ahead to request scripts/appointments)
www.library.ucla.edu/yrl

Museum of Television and Radio

465 N. Beverly Drive
Beverly Hills, CA 90210
(310) 786–1025
www.mtr.org

25 West 52nd Street
New York, NY 10019
(212) 621–6800
www.mtr.org

Where to Get Scripts

You can try getting scripts directly from the show. Go to *Variety* online and sign up for a free 14-day membership. Then select Charts and Data, TV Production, and you will be able to get a list of TV shows that are currently in production and the phone numbers to contact the production offices. No guarantee, but you might get lucky.

You can also go to fan sites for whatever show you're looking for and find episode synopses and scripts—though often they are not production scripts, which is what you need: they are transcripts, which don't do you much good. Best source for scripts are other writers who have been able to get copies through agents or friends who've worked on the show.

Here are some sources that have production scripts, which you can buy for many current and most old TV shows:

www.planetmegamall.com

www.dailyscript.com/tv.html

www.simplyscripts.com/tv.html

www.script-o-rama.com/snazzy/dircut.html

www.scriptcity.net

www.bookcity.net

The Writers Guild Library has hundreds of television scripts available; however, you must read them at the library. You cannot check them out or copy them.

Publications of Specific Interest to Writers

Creative Screenwriting—CS Weekly shows up weekly in your email box. It's a digest version of *Creative Screenwriting* magazine. You can subscribe at the Creative Screenwriting website: www.creativescreenwriting.com/csdaily.html

Written By—magazine of the Writers Guild. Available to nonmembers by subscription or on a few newsstands in L.A. Back issues are available online at the Writers Guild website: http://www.wga.org/writtenby/writtenby.aspx

NATPE DailyLead—online headline service. Focus is on television news and, as it says, it's daily. natpe@dailylead.com

newsfeed@mediabistro.com—another daily online update, focus is on magazines and publishing.

Cynthia Turner Synopsis—Daily online headline service from Warner Bros., so it's heavy on the promo for Warner product; focus is TV and often duplicates NATPE DailyLead. cynthia@cynopsis.com

The Trades

Hollywood Reporter
www.hollywoodreporter.com

Variety
www.variety.com

Variety and the *Hollywood Reporter* are called "the trades" and are available both online and by subscription. It's not exactly in-depth reporting, as it's mostly press release announcements about what's in the works. You'll find the ratings in the trades and announcements of new pilots, what shows have been canceled, and which actors have been signed to pilot deals. If you want insight into what's going on in Hollywood, I recommend the business section of the *New York Times*. There are frequent articles on the corporate workings of the studios and networks and, of course, all the latest on executive lawsuits.

Many people maintain that you must read the trades every day to stay current about trends and the business. I don't suppose it could hurt, although it's seductive to get caught up in the hype of celebrity deals and the excitement of the big numbers (or it might be depressing to read about everybody else's six-figure deals every day). While I certainly agree you ought to have some working knowledge about what is getting bought and sold and how the marketplace works, I think your main focus is best kept on the actual work you do: the writing.

Useful Websites

Writers Guild of America, West
www.wga.org

www.mediabistro.com—a website and daily email with classes, publishing, showbiz headlines, and many job listings, often entry-level assistants and intern positions.

Hollywood Creative Directory
www.hcdonline.com

Internet Movie Database
www.imdb.com

UCLA Extension Writers' Program
www.unex.ucla.edu/writers

www.showbizjobs.com—a random check of this website shows three jobs for agent's assistants and one for a paid production assistant on a small movie.

www.nielsenmedia.com—Nielsen ratings

www.tvtracker.com—for in-depth analysis of ratings and other current TV information

www.tv.com—TV information that is more fan oriented than TV tracker

www.tvtickets.com—to get tickets for TV tapings

www.whorepresents.com—how to contact people

www.janeespenson.com—fun blog by a working writer

www.scriptwritersnetwork.com—writers' networking and support group that has monthly gatherings with speakers

www.emmys.org—Academy of Television Arts & Sciences

www.copyright.gov—U.S. Copyright Office, 101 Independence
Ave. SE, Washington, DC 20559–6000, (202) 707–3000

Recommended for the Writer's Library

There are many excellent books on writing and you can find recommendations online and in bookstores if you haven't already. The books I'm recommending here are a few personal favorites, not on the usual Top 10 Lists. Many of them are not specifically directed at scriptwriting, but I've found them especially helpful and I'd like to pass them along to you, both for your pleasure and as a thank-you to the authors for providing me with inspiration and guidance.

You Must Have:

A Dictionary—not the spell-check in your computer, or even the dictionary in your computer. An actual book, a big one with etymology and synonyms, and archaic usages that you can roam around in and see more than just the word you're looking up. Words are your business.

Susan Beavers, the showrunner of *Dudley*, a show I worked

for, gave all the writers on staff the *Random House Dictionary of the English Language*. Unabridged edition, 2,400+ pages. The show was gone after six episodes, but that dictionary is still on my desk and I use it almost every day. Some days lifting it is the most exercise I get.

A Thesaurus—also an actual book, for the same reasons as the dictionary. These are your basic writer's tools. They should sit on your desk so you look at (and in) them all the time.

You Should Have:

Scripts—TV and film. As many as you can collect, and do read them.

Plays—one acts and full length.

A daily newspaper besides the trades. You need to stay in touch with the world, not just showbiz—the fads, the fashions, the opinions, the fears, and the events. If you don't, you'll just wind up writing about what you saw on TV, and there's way too much of that already.

A script-formatting guide. Either *The Complete Guide to Standard Script Formats* by Cole/Haag or *The Screenwriter's Bible* by David Trottier. They are both on my desk, right next to that enormous dictionary.

You'll Be Glad You Have:

The Elements of Style, William Strunk & E. B. White—a small but mighty bible for anyone who writes.

Becoming a Writer, Dorothea Brande—both practical and inspirational. Written in 1934, before there even was such a thing as television, but every word applies.

On Writing Well, William Zinsser—for journalists, but an excellent guide to writing in general; pay particular attention to Chapter 2, Simplicity.

Respect for Acting, Uta Hagen—Ms. Hagen was my acting teacher when I began my career working in the theater. I have used what I learned from her in more ways than I can count. Her book is addressed to actors, but it's an invaluable guide for anyone who writes for actors as well. You can see Ms. Hagen in action on the video *Uta Hagen's Acting Class.* Available from several sources online.

The Comedy Bible, Judy Carter—covers all kinds of comedy writing. A good resource whether you're writing comedy or drama.

The Eight Characters of Comedy, Scott Sedita—great examples and detailed guidance on how to structure comedy that comes from character.

> Take the first step in faith. You don't have to see the whole staircase, just take the first step.
> —DR. MARTIN LUTHER KING JR.

Index

Author's Note

Thank you for buying my book. If you have any comments about the book, suggestions for the next edition, or if you'd like to ask me anything about what you've read in the book, please go to my website (www.SandlerInk.com) and you'll find a link to email me. I'll be happy to hear from you.

Ellen Sandler received an Emmy nomination for her work as Co-Executive Producer for the CBS hit comedy *Everybody Loves Raymond*. She has worked as a writer/producer for many other network television shows including ABC's long-running series, *Coach*. In addition, she has created original pilots for ABC, CBS, NBC, Fox Family, Oxygen, The Disney Channel and the Australian Children's Television Foundation in Melbourne, Australia.

She teaches writing for the UCLA Extension Writer's Program, MediaBistro, The HB Playwrights Foundation, and The New School in New York. Through her consulting company, Sandler Ink, she provides script development and career coaching for professionals and emerging writers in the entertainment industry. Ellen is a member of the Writers Guild of America, a graduate of Syracuse University, and holds an MFA in filmmaking from the American Film Institute.